D0342680

Advance Praise for *Wannabe: Gangs in Suburbs and Schools*:

"Dr Dan Monti's study of the Fairview School District was an in-depth and a revealing description of the impact of gangs on school-age youth and the school environment. It is more evident to us and other suburban school districts that no one is isolated from gang or gang-like activities among youths. It served as a 'wake up' call for our school district and required us to get busy and develop plans to counter the negative effects of gang activity. Read and take heed, this is happening in your school district."

Superintendent, Fairview School District

". . . well written, very interesting, and certainly of great importance in understanding how our society is to deal with some of its most intractable problems. I was struck by the fact that gangs serve as a focus of identity for those who join them, not because it is a new idea, but because our schools have been systematically stripped of any affective qualities – anything that might provide an alternative sense of identity."

Diane Ravitch, The Brookings Institution

"Professor Monti sees clearly that gang problems are *not* reducible to problems of poverty, ethnicity, color, or other accidents of birth and circumstance. The existence of gangs, he argues, does not signify a morally bankrupt or racist nation: 'Perhaps we finally are ready to see youth violence and drug dealing as challenges to the rights and responsibilities that come with one's membership in this society.'"

Edwin J. Delattre, Boston

"*Wannabe* is a poignant reminder of just how difficult it will be to develop public policy designed to control the 'youth gangs' which so terrorize both urban and suburban neighborhoods. Dan Monti's contribution is the brutal honesty of his work. The words, however, are not his own. He lets the gang-bangers and wannabes tell their stories. Chilling stories, 'out of the mouths of babes', about children and young adults who moonlight as organized criminals and contract killers. God Help us! We will need it."

Robert Destro
Catholic University School of Law
Former member United States Commission on Civil Rights

Wannabe
Gangs in Suburbs and Schools

Daniel J. Monti

NATIONAL UNIVERSITY
LIBRARY LOS ANGELES

BLACKWELL
Oxford UK & Cambridge USA

Copyright © Daniel J. Monti, 1994

The right of Daniel J. Monti to be identified as author of this work has been asserted in accordance with the Copyright, Designs and Patents Act 1988.

Blackwell Publishers
238 Main Street
Cambridge, Massachusetts 02142
USA

108 Cowley Road
Oxford OX4 1JF
UK

All rights reserved. Except for the quotation of short passages for the purposes of criticism and review, no part of this publication may be reproduced, stored in a retrieval system, or transmitted, in any form or by any means, electronic, mechanical, photocopying, recording or otherwise, without the prior permission of the publisher.

Except in the United States of America, this book is sold subject to the condition that it shall not, by way of trade or otherwise, be lent, resold, hired out, or otherwise circulated without the publisher's prior consent in any form of binding or cover other than that in which it is published and without a similar condition including this condition being imposed on the subsequent purchaser.

Library of Congress Cataloging-in-Publication Data
Monti, Daniel J.
    Wannabe : gangs in suburbs and schools /
Daniel J. Monti.
        p.   cm.
    Includes bibliographical references.
    ISBN 1–55786–614–7 (alk. paper). – ISBN 1–55786–615–5 (pbk.
alk. paper)
    1. Gangs – United States.   2. Suburbs – United States.   I. Title.
HV6439.U5M65   1994
364.1′06′0973 – dc20   94–7851
                                                                                    CIP

British Library Cataloguing in Publication Data

A CIP catalogue record for this book is available from the British Library.

Typeset in 11 on 12 pt Bembo
by Colset Private Limited, Singapore
Printed and Bound in Great Britain by
Hartnolls Limited, Bodmin, Cornwall.

This book is printed on acid-free paper

Contents

Foreword

Much of the research, quasi-research, and popular literature of the past fifty years or so on gangs contains arresting, even riveting, descriptive material. Books, articles, media stories on gangs – whether prepared by scholars, journalists, social workers, law enforcement personnel, or reformed gang members – contain transcribed interviews with gang members and wannabes that confirm much that has been understood about human nature and the springs of human action for thousands of years. Daniel Monti's *Wannabe: Gangs in Suburbs and Schools* is no exception.

Unfortunately, many putative authorities (wannabes of another sort) on gangs and gang-related phenomena are naive. Clever gang members hoodwink them, and the writers, in their gullibility, pass misinformation along to the public. Not so, Professor Monti. With other fine teachers, he often likes the young people he comes to know, but he never sentimentalizes them either in the particular or in the abstract. Though he understands that the young sometimes try to appear immutable precisely because they are not, he also knows how to ask questions and to listen with a concentration that may draw a young person toward reflectiveness.

Professor Monti never assumes reflectiveness in the young people he interviews. Still, he sometimes discovers it. He does not ascribe to them a self-knowledge they never had. He knows that assertive certitude, even sincerity, is no more evidence of self-knowledge or accurate reporting by a gangbanger than by anyone else. For these reasons, and because he does not suppose that any of us can easily know all of our own motives, Professor Monti is spared the error of other researchers and writers who believe that initial personal testimony is bound to be autobiographically revealing and decisive.

"Most researchers," he writes, "lead one to believe that these youngsters adopt an identity as a gang member and then push on their merry way." By contrast, Professor Monti finds that some of the young people in his study actively think about gang life, worry about choices they are making, and feel real fears that they are willing, in some contexts, to talk about.

At the same time, Daniel Monti has acquired a discerning eye for recognizing the youngster who is pathological, psychopathic, potentially murderous. He has the respect for reality that enables him to face up to genuine evil when he encounters it. Of an interview with fifth grader "Yancey Vardar," Professor Monti writes: "We talked a while longer, but it was hard for me. It was not that he said anything particularly shocking . . . He presented his sentences in a clipped and practiced way that I found unnerving. There was no light in this child, no feeling. He was cold, and he frightened me."

Monti was right to be unnerved and frightened. When he uncharacteristically told a counselor that Vardar was a "murder waiting to happen," the counselor confided that Vardar had progressed from killing birds and small animals with an air rifle to shooting other children, first in the ankles, then higher up the legs. "He's practicing how to kill," Monti inferred, and unless someone killed him first, he would almost surely "end up killing someone because he liked it."

Professor Monti acknowledges that some children, formed almost entirely by gang culture that glorifies violence, are largely beyond our reach, beyond reform. This distinguishes him from foolish optimists who believe that malevolent habits of feeling, thought, and action are always reversible. Professor Monti understands that predators resemble all the rest of us in the sense that they like the habits they acquire. Those who acquire a taste for inflicting suffering on others frequently never get over it and never have any desire to get over it. True remorselessness runs bone deep.

Many who write about gangs have never studied history in any depth. They do not grasp that human motives which figure in gang membership and the emergence of gangs have long been recognized for their power in other forms of human association. These motives range from benign and hopeful yearnings for meaning, order, and identity, to more frightening forms of loneliness and desperation; and from poverty of imagination, resentment, rage, lust, and the will to dominate, to sterile ambition, self-contempt, hatred, and deep malevolence toward others. Professor Monti has studied history.

It should come as no surprise, then, that he has not chased the media, which have chased ambulances, into the inner cities to find gangs. Understanding that human beings, including the young, are routinely motivated by the same sorts of yearnings and desires, and remain susceptible to the same sorts of temptations despite differences in their circumstances, Professor Monti has turned toward gang activity in the suburbs. He draws his readers toward thoughtfulness about the fact that we and our children are inevitably social beings, however antisocial our forms of association may become. His clarity about the relevance of human nature frees him, and his readers, from the errors of writers on gangs who suppose that they can reach "root causes" of gang phenomena by looking only at particular kinds of localized social conditions.

Professor Monti writes, "When places as different as inner-city slums and suburban townships have gangs, one must submit that either persons in both places share the same values and moral vision or that their unique views about what is right or wrong cannot tell us much about where gangs will develop. I prefer the latter explanation." There is more to the story, of course. In the Los Angeles riots after the Simi Valley acquittal of Los Angeles police officers indicted for beating motorist Rodney King, many people who were arrested for looting in the second day of disorder – grandparents, parents, children – explained that they had seen people on television looting with impunity. They imitated what they watched. All of us are creatures of imitation, and what children witness, and imitate, is by no means confined to their own neighborhoods. Through the media, everyone sees many of the same things.

Patterns of imitation – with patterns of entertainment – transcend economics, ethnicity, color, and geography. "Gangsta" rap music enjoys huge popularity with suburban teenage audiences. And suburbanites go to inner cities. They go there to buy drugs and narcotics, as anyone who spends time near the open-air drug markets of our cities and watches traffic patterns can see. Suburbanites also go to inner cities to buy sex from prostitutes. This helps to explain, for example, the thousands of new cases of syphilis reported in 1992 in suburban Chicago. Our suburbs are not nearly as insular as many who live there believe.

Wannabe is a book well suited to a wide public readership. But because it is rooted in an understanding of history and human nature, it is much more intellectually substantial than a great deal of research literature prepared for specialists. It has another advantage. Professor Monti does not confuse being objective with being nonjudgmental about human excellence, mediocrity, and depravity. Thus, he does not fear normative discourse: "Children are not supposed to act this way. Their lives ought not to be shaped by the customary rhythms of drug deals and brawls ... It is an outrage that they fight and kill each other with dangerous weapons."

Still, Professor Monti does not subject his readers to the "obligatory" concluding chapter of the gang literature genre that consists of prescriptions for reform. Often these prescriptions amount to no more than empty platitudes and utopian speculations. Instead, he argues – as James Madison argued in *Federalist #10* – that because factions cannot be eradicated (the cure is worse than the affliction), the question is how to control the violence of faction: "If gangs are not going away and tolerating their activities is not a viable option, then we will have to find ways to limit the impact they have on us." And he rightly insists that if we leave our children to their own devices, absent our loving and sustained attention to them and to the formation of their character, gangs will exploit the situation we create. These *really* are *our* children – and no one else's efforts in their behalf can replace our own sacrifices for their sake, our own concerted investment in their lives and their formation.

Professor Monti sees clearly that gang problems are *not* reducible to problems of poverty, ethnicity, color, or other accidents of birth and circumstance. The existence of gangs, he argues, does not signify a morally bankrupt or racist nation: "Perhaps we finally are ready to see youth violence and drug dealing as challenges to the rights and responsibilities that come with one's membership in this society."

We share the conviction that gangs – in all their variety and ranging from those that arise out of boredom (the "shriek of unused capacity," Saul Bellow calls it) to the deeply malevolent criminal conspiracies that turn neighborhoods into war zones – are not somebody else's problem. Gang phenomena, the emergence of children as predators who like the mean and destructive habits they acquire, the pathological glorification of power and riches: all of these are *our* problems as parents, as citizens, as adults.

Edwin J. Delattre
Boston, Massachusetts

Acknowledgments

The children and young men and women portrayed in this book live in the suburbs of a mid-western city in the United States and attend school in a place that I have chosen to call the Fairview School District. I told them that nothing they shared with me would bring trouble to them, and that is why I did not use their names, the names of school personnel, or the real names of their schools and towns. I have masked their identities as best I could and used their words lavishly in the hope that anyone who reads this book would understand how vulnerable the young persons portrayed in it are and how deeply I am indebted to them. I hope that readers will respect the commitment I made to the four hundred or more boys and girls who spoke with me and shared an important part of their life with me.

I made no such promise to the young adults who travel from larger cities like Los Angeles and Chicago to places like the Fairview School District in order to entice these same boys and girls to sell narcotic substances. Nor do I feel any commitment to their customers, adults who are stupid or desperate enough to ingest the drugs they sell, or to adults who are willing to look the other way while this happens. We are beyond forgiving and are deserving of the contempt that the children in this book express for us.

As for myself, I will say only that I am grateful for all the trust invested in me by the administrators and students of the Fairview School District. You were good and honest teachers. Beyond that it is important to know that while I am responsible for every word on these pages, whatever insight they may reflect is a tribute to my teachers. The errors are mine alone.

The author thanks the editors of *Qualitative Sociology*, Vol. 16, No. 4 (Winter 1993): 383–404 for publishing some material from chapter five.

Boston

Introduction

It really helps to like young people when you do research on a subject like gangs, because sometimes teenagers are little shits. They can work hard at making themselves unlikeable and succeed handsomely at it. One such soul had just left the room where I was working. At the age of sixteen he was full of himself and tough as a tack. We had jousted a while and tried to make sense of all that I had learned about gangs in his suburban school district, but nothing much had come of it. I managed to soften him a bit and even had him concede an obvious and important fact about himself. He was a gangbanger, and he liked it. Beyond that, however, he was willing to offer little information about what it was he did as a gang member and how he made sense of it. We left on good terms, having convinced each other that neither of us had horns or was likely to grow them any time soon.

It really did not matter. I had been interviewing students at the high school for nearly four weeks and had learned a great deal. My chart showing the size and distribution of gangs in the Fairview School District was shaping up nicely. There were a few details about the organization and behavior of certain gangs that I wanted to acquire, but I was growing weary of the place and of my own little routine. Besides, it was early spring, the school year was almost over, and the stories about gang fights and drug dealing had grown all too familiar.

"How do you know when you've talked to enough people?" an incredulous pollster once asked me.

"Easy," I responded. "You know when you stop getting new stories."

For several years I had been interviewing youngsters in the city bordering the Fairview School District. I had come to know when there was little left to learn about a young person's gang or his involvement with it. Sure, you could hang around and pretend that you were blending into their world and let them pretend that they were showing you more than they already had told you or would never tell you out loud. However, there was just so much that they could or would tell you unless you were one of them. I was not stupid or reckless enough to carry out such a pretense, and I respected them too much to try.[1] Furthermore, it did not take long to figure out that most of these youngsters had not tried to make sense of much that they did as gangbangers. It was not that they were thoughtless, but that they were merely unreflective. My questions more often were received with bemused silence than hostility. Whatever insight many of them left an interview with was constructed during the interview. They had not brought it into the room.

I had reached the point at the Fairview School District when I was getting no new stories. New bits of information had been coming much less frequently, and whatever themes or patterns were going to emerge from my interviews had already appeared. I was tidying up, trying hard to convince myself that I really should meet with the last seven students on my list.

I glanced out the window of the conference room that doubled as a cabinet for the central office staff. "Groan," I muttered to myself. "She did it again."

Two students were sitting on a bench at the end of the corridor that led to my makeshift office. They were waiting for me to call them. I had asked the secretary not to bring students down to the office until I was ready for them. This proved to be quite difficult at the high school for reasons that never were clear to me.

I did not like taking them from classes and making them wait for me, even though many students enjoyed leaving classes they thought were boring. They were being schooled, but neither they nor the principal were certain about the education part. I also feared that sooner or later youngsters from different "groups" would be put together and start fighting. That had not happened yet in any school I had visited, and I did not want it to happen now with my work nearly completed.

I need not have worried. These two seemed to know each other and were chatting amiably. "Oh well," I thought. "Two down and five to go."

I beckoned the older student to join me. He rose and walked down the corridor.

He was taller than I, a good two or three inches beyond six feet, and slim. His hair was cut close, and his dark skin was complemented by the brown trousers and patterned shirt that he wore. The top two or three buttons on his shirt were open, revealing no chains hanging around his neck. In fact, the only jewelry he wore was a rather modest wrist watch.

I glanced down at my list. His name was Tyrone Jones.

There was nothing fancy about Tyrone Jones. Nevertheless, he carried himself well and had the look of someone who was ready to graduate and move beyond high school. "Another one of the principal's pet students," I said to myself.

I greeted him at the door and directed him to a seat close to my own. I closed the door behind him, and we both took our seats. I began "the speech."

"My name is Dan Monti, and I teach at the university."

He knew that. Hell, everybody knew that. Even in a school with fifteen hundred students like Fairview High, a stranger stuck out. An adult with a beard who asked questions about gangs and drugs was a mobile billboard with great name recognition. Moreover, I had been interviewing students across the district since September and it was now early April. Word of who I was and what I was doing had long ago reached the high school. It probably had come from the junior high school where the students had tagged me "the Sicilian." They had routine contact with the students at the high school through their families, neighborhoods, and gangs. Word of my work also could have come from the elementary schools, but that was less likely. There I was known as "Lead Butt," an equally accurate and flattering sobriquet offered by the school counselors who sat in on all my interviews. If Tyrone Jones had not heard about me from those sources, he surely would have learned who I was within my first two days at the high school.

Tyrone Jones knew who I was and why I was there, all right. He was not the least bit surprised by my opening line. Nor had he appeared particularly impressed. No matter. By my rough estimate just over four hundred youngsters in the Fairview School District had heard "the speech" since September. There was no reason for Tyrone not to hear it, too.

"I've been visiting all the schools in the District."

This was not quite true. The Fairview School District has eleven schools. I interviewed students in only ten of them. One elementary school had no fifth or sixth grade, and my early interviews with children younger than ten years old had satisfied me that in this district at least, little would be gained by talking to the youngest children. They knew little about drugs and even less about gangs, other than what they had learned from the television or movies. I decided not to interview anyone at that school. District officials supported that decision and, indeed, had predicted that nothing much would be learned from their youngest charges. It was, in any case, easier to say what I said than to explain several hundred times why I had not visited one elementary school.

"And I've been talking to a great many students about gangs and drugs in the Fairview School District."

I had been given unprecedented access to any and all students in the district. I could ask to meet with any student, and staff at each school would see to it that the youngster was called to the room where I was located.

In the elementary schools, this was the counselor's office. In the junior and senior high schools, it was a conference room near the offices of the school's vice principals. This was done as a matter of convenience for me and the office staff who were responsible for gathering those students I requested to meet.

Some students were concerned that they had been called to the school counselor or vice principal's office. They wondered whether they had done something wrong. This was particularly so in the case of junior and senior high school students who knew the vice principals to be the school's chief disciplinarians. With this in mind, I took great care in the latter portions of "the speech" to assure students that they had done nothing wrong and were in no danger of being punished for any past transgression. This seemed to reassure most of them. Those who had doubts or expressed any reservations were excused from the interview. Few made such concerns obvious or took advantage of the offer to end the interview before I had a chance to ask any questions.[2]

"I'm not trying to get anyone in trouble. I'm just trying to figure out what's going on in the schools and community."

My object had been to discover how many, if any, gangs were operating in and around the Fairview School District. I also wanted to learn as much as I could about how gangs were organized and what gangs did in the suburbs and schools. I knew that my work would provide fresh insights into these matters because there were no studies of gangs in suburbs and only a few references to what gangs did in schools.

I had no interest in finding out who all the gang members were in a particular school or in cataloguing their various adventures and misdeeds. At first, I was not curious about what motivated young men and women to become gang members or how they made sense of what they were doing. I did not care to play amateur psychologist and crawl into their heads until I was able to tick off a list of the reasons they had become gangbangers.

I had read many studies in which adults speculated about why a youngster became a gang member, and I did not want to contribute to their half-baked theories. They treated all children as if they were the same, driven by real or imagined demons that dwell in the minds of persons reared in slums. They painted a picture of children as twisted, thoughtless, and reckless beings who rambled on the edges of civilized society with little hope for themselves and even less concern for the well-being of others. I wanted no part of this research. I thought it as dangerous as the children portrayed in it, because other adults no doubt read and believed this social scientific claptrap.

My only scholarly interest in these students initially, then, was as gatekeepers to the groups they had observed or to which they belonged. I became more drawn to how they made themselves into gang members and why they left gangs only after listening to many of them reflect on their own experiences. These were not like the children about whom so much drivel had been written. They could have been my children.

"But before I start asking you questions there are a couple of things that you should know. First, you're not in any trouble. You did nothing wrong to be asked to meet with me. The principal or counselors just thought you might be someone who was knowledgeable about gangs and drugs."

I did not select the first bunch of students that I interviewed at each school. Principals were requested to provide me with a list of students who might know something about gangs and drugs. Without exception, each principal submitted a list that had between twenty and thirty names on it. Insofar as these lists constituted an honest attempt on the part of the principals to comply with my request, the elementary school principals thought that a greater share of their students was knowledgeable about these matters than did the junior and senior high school principals.[3] I found this curious.

The students on these original lists were asked to suggest other youngsters who they thought might know something about gangs and drugs. No one was asked to say whether the person they had suggested was, in fact, a gang member or drug dealer. Children in the elementary schools provided some names that were not on my original list. More often, however, they identified students with whom we planned to meet. The situation was very different in the junior and senior high schools. The students in these schools added many names to my list. Indeed, they provided up to three times as many names as had been offered by school staff. Moreover, the individuals suggested by their fellow students always were well informed about specific gangs and what gangs did.

One might have concluded that the elementary school principals and counselors were smarter, better attuned to what was going on in their schools, and/or more honest than the principals in the junior and senior high schools. There was some truth to this. Still, a number of elementary school children brought in for interviews had little firsthand information about gangs and drugs. On the other hand, virtually all of the students identified by junior and senior high school staff possessed relevant information. The most likely explanation for the dramatic under-reporting of potential informants at the junior and senior high schools was suggested by elementary school staff: the building administrators at the junior and senior high schools did not want to acknowledge the existence of a gang or drug problem at their schools. I found this to be a pretty accurate perception.

"Second, nothing you say in this room is going to get you in trouble. I may use what you tell me in a report that I'm going to make to the superintendent or a book, but no one will know what you told me unless you tell them."

I guaranteed the anonymity of my subjects. I had found over many years that this was the only and best way to ensure that I received good information. I always ran the risk of being lied to during the course of an interview. Furthermore, most persons can be expected to exaggerate at least some of the details in their stories. I acquired a good sense of when I was being lied to or "fed a line," however. I also had discovered some years ago that most persons are not particularly adept at lying and work harder at embellishing a story than they do at telling the truth. In any case, the assurance that their words would not come back to haunt them had a salutary effect. The students told me what they knew, and usually made it apparent when their information had come from another source or was merely gossip or speculation.

"Third, if you have a problem with any of the questions I ask, we can talk about it. If you still have a problem with any question after hearing my explanation, you don't have to answer it. In fact, you can end this interview at any time, pick up your books, and return to your class."

I paused for a moment and looked for a reaction from Tyrone. There was none. He sat calmly with his hands resting gently on the table. He was looking at me, but in a somewhat detached way. I could continue.

Most students had no problem with either the interview format or the questions they were asked. This was a compliment to the adults who had helped to put the project together. We had tried to put the interests of the students above our concern for getting the most information we could squeeze from them, and I believe that we had succeeded. The fact is, however, that the ultimate responsibility for acquiring information and behaving fairly was mine.

Most people could not do this kind of work, and few would enjoy it. It is hard to sit for hours and listen to a succession of stories that may or may not have any common theme running through them. It is harder yet to be introduced to some meaner sides of the human spirit through the eyes and words of children. You gain access to their world by virtue of who you are and how you present yourself. There are many times when you wish that you had not done quite so good a job at entering their world, and none of those occasions has anything to do with the fine art of making a tough kid back off without having to threaten him. It has everything to do with getting information and gaining insight without giving pain. There are times when I truly hate what I learn, but I believe that some larger purpose will be served by my telling of their story. In the end, I simply try to be fair.

This is sometimes harder to accomplish than one might think. In the case of my work in the Fairview School District, for instance, we did not treat elementary school children in the same way that we treated junior and senior high school students. Letters were sent home to the parents of all elementary school students indicating that their child might be interviewed about gang and drug problems. (We assumed that a responsible adult in the household could read and would read the letter. There are many settings in which the presumption of parental literacy could not be so easily made, but we were pretty certain that the parents of our children could read. We were less certain that they might take the time to read the letter, but we decided not to make that our problem.) Parents were invited to write the principal of their child's school, if they objected to having such an interview take place. Only one or two parents from each school did so, and their child was not interviewed.

There was one exception. A new teacher in one school took it upon herself to contact the parents of her pupils and encouraged them not to cooperate with the study. A good number of them complied with that suggestion. No effort was made to change their minds, but I made my displeasure clear to school administrators.

I had not anticipated this problem. I had met with staff from the elementary schools the previous spring and thought that I had answered all their questions about the study at that time. Apparently I was wrong. It was clear in retrospect that I should have been reintroduced to the staff at each school just before I began my interviews or that the school principal should have assumed more responsibility in smoothing my way into his or her school. For whatever reason, this did not happen at one school and my work there was frustrated because of it.

I took no exception to a second concession made to the younger children. School administrators decided after only a little discussion that the school counselor would participate in all interviews with pupils from that school. No one thought that I would mistreat the children. All of us simply wanted to be certain that no one could truthfully say that these young children had been subjected to any undue pressure during the interview. None was. Moreover, I actually appreciated having the counselor present in most cases. It helped to establish a good and supportive atmosphere for these younger children and provided a second adult who could and did say, "Yes, that's what they're telling us."

None of us thought that such precautions needed to be taken when it came to working with junior and senior high school students. We all assumed that these students were mature enough to decide whether they would consent to be interviewed. Only a few youngsters from each school expressed any reluctance to speak with me, and many were eager to share what they knew about gangs and drug dealing.

Tyrone Jones who sat next to me now appeared neither eager nor unwilling to talk with me. He simply waited patiently for me to finish what I had to say. He was a good example of why older students could be expected to do what they believed was in their own best interest. In the case of Tyrone, I was beginning to think that he might not be another of the principal's ringers, a member of the group called "A Few Good Men" that the principal had pulled together to serve as "positive role models" for other students in the wake of fights between "boys from different towns."

The principal of the school, Dwayne Turner, had packed his list of prospective interview subjects with members of "A Few Good Men". He had cooperated with the project, but he also had assured me that there was no serious gang problem in his school. I assumed that his "Few Good Men" were supposed to convince me that was so, but they had provided a great deal of useful information and suggested a number of other students with whom I should speak. One or two also had dropped tantalizing hints about how hard it was sometimes to know who the real gang members were and that their teachers would be terribly surprised, if they knew who was "slangin," or selling, cocaine and crack.

These students had touched on another reason why I had not wanted the parents of older students contacted about the possibility of their child being interviewed. I knew that many parents were unaware of their child's involvement with gangs or drugs. Anything that alerted them to such entanglements might well jeopardize the child's relationship with his or her parents. I also knew that some parents sold drugs, and I did not want them to believe that something their child might say would put them at risk. It was better to allow the young women and men with whom I spoke to control what they would tell me.

I glanced again at Tyrone Jones before continuing with my presentation and studied his patient face. He had clear, dark eyes that allowed little to escape their attention; but there also was something sad about his eyes, as if they should have been in an older body. My opinion of him was changing, and he had said nothing beyond our initial exchange of pleasantries at the start of our meeting. "This kid's no pet of the principal's," I thought. "He's got something to tell me."

"Fourth, I don't want to hear about a specific crime that anyone, including you, might have committed. No names. No dates. No places. If you give me the name of someone who committed a particular crime, then I'm going to stop my tape recorder and wipe it out."

While I was certain that teenagers would act in a self-interested way, I was less sure that they had enough self-knowledge to protect themselves on all occasions. I did not want them to blurt out information that, on reflection, they would see might put them at a disadvantage. So I took this small precaution to assure them that I was aware of their interests at those moments when they were not as careful as they should have been with what they said.

It was rare that a person I was interviewing injected someone's name into the story he was telling, but it did happen. Most of the time we both would catch it. The student would pause and shake his head or roll his eyes, while

I erased that part of the tape where a name had been mentioned. There were occasions, however, when both of us were so involved in our discussion that we failed to notice that another person had been named in relation to a particular crime. I caught this error when transcribing my tape-recorded conversations and erased it from the tape at that time.

Something far more interesting happened most of the time, particularly among junior and senior high school students. In the early part of our conversations, students were much more likely to speak in the third person or use indefinite or subjunctive verb forms when talking about events and impressions that clearly were their own. They would say, "He sold drugs" or "That group might want to take over someone else's territory." Somewhat later in our discussions, when I presume they were more comfortable or at least less guarded, students often switched their mode of speaking and used first-person pronouns and more active verb forms. They would say, "I sell" or "My gang is going to take over their territory." I was surprised at how many students did this. Students who remained guarded stuck with language that put them at arm's length from the persons or events they were describing.

Only a few students were reluctant to have any part or all of their conversation with me tape-recorded. These students did allow me to take notes on a pad of paper. Most young persons, unlike adults I have interviewed, do not mind having their voices copied.

"Fifth, if you tell me about something bad that is going to happen in school or out of school, like a fight or drug deal going down at a particular time and place, I will report it to the proper authorities. They will not be told, of course, who informed me of the event. That stays in this room."

No student used the interview as an opportunity to warn me of something that was about to happen. I had the impression, though, that they appreciated my candor and willingness to set limits on what I was willing to do, or not do, with the information they gave me. It protected both of us.

The necessity of having such a rule of engagement had first been driven home to me in an earlier project when someone informed me of a contract killing that was allegedly going to take place. On that occasion, I contacted local and federal law enforcement officials and did my best to arrange for the intended target to receive some protection. It did not stop the shooting from taking place; but it did alert me to the potential hazards of becoming too involved with my subjects.

I looked at Tyrone Jones and asked, "Do you have any questions?"

He did. It was: "Where did you say this information was going?"

"I've been asked by the Superintendent to find out what's going on with gangs and drugs in the Fairview School District. I'm going to write a report for him summarizing what students have told me. After that, I don't know where I'll write it up. Right now I'm trying to put together a chart that shows how many gangs are out there, how large they are, and which ones are fighting or friendly with each other."

I pushed two pieces of paper in front of him. The first one had on it the names, sizes, and "alliances" of the fourteen known male gangs in the Fairview School District. The second one contained comparable information on the five known female gangs. He looked at the page with the male gangs arranged in two broad coalitions. One set was loosely aligned with different Crips out of Los Angeles. The other collection of gangs was tied to a variety of Bloods from Los Angeles. He nodded in agreement with most of the information presented in the chart, but he took a pencil and changed the number of persons belonging to one particular gang roughly allied with the Crips. "That's better," he said.

He turned to the chart showing female gangs. He looked at it briefly and laughed. "What's so funny?" I asked.

He shook his head gently and said, "Those Banister Bitches. Just a group of snotty-nosed girls think they're hard."

I nodded my head and tried to direct his attention back to the male gang whose membership numbers he had adjusted. This was the one gang that was reputed to have no fixed geographic territory or turf that it called "home," and I had not found out too much about it.

"There are Disciples in the Fairview area?" I asked.

His answer was short and firm. "Right."

He had noted on the chart that there were fifty members of the Disciples in this area. "Is this a good estimate?" I wondered aloud.

"Better than that," he responded.

"How old are they?"

"Well, there are six 'Kings.' They're between nineteen and twenty years old. Under them come the 'Supreme Violators' who are between sixteen and eighteen years old. It varies at different schools. Here there are two. Under them are the 'Chief Violators.' They're the same age [as the Supreme Violators]. There's one at this school."

He paused for a moment and then continued, "Then there are the 'Shorty Recruiters' who are between thirteen and eighteen years old. They're working their way up. There are two here."

"How many of these persons have been formally initiated?"

"Three of the Kings are 'made.' The rest are 'wannabes.'"

"How does one move up in the organization?"

"To move up a rank you have to fight two from the level above you."

I interrupted him at that point. "You know that community-based gangs are very strong here."

"Right."

"Don't any of the Disciples also belong to neighborhood gangs?"

"No," he replied. "You can't be a pancake. You can't flip from one gang to another. If they catch you doin' that, I feel sorry for you. They'll make you walk the line." (The offending party would walk between two parallel lines of his fellow Disciples and be administered a terrific beating as he proceeded from one end to the other.)

"Maybe so," I replied. "But these recruits live in the community. Are you telling me that they won't help other boys from their own town?"

"No. They'll go down in a fight with the kids from their hood, but they won't join that gang."

"How much do the Disciple members do as a group?"

"Most everything they do, they do together."

"Including selling dope?"

"Yeah. Somewhat."

"How much dealing is there?"

"I know one at this school who deals in kilos. He only sells kilos and half kilos."

"To whom does he sell it?"

"Disciples won't sell to their own. They'll sell it to someone else."

"What do you mean?"

"He won't sell it to any black people here, but he will sell it to the white kids [in the wealthy suburbs]. You see, Disciples is more like a black militant group. They don't believe in destroyin' each other; but they'll sell it to the other man and let them destroy them own selves."

"But what about those Disciples who are white?"

"Just because they're a Disciple doesn't mean they'll deal."

"How many at the high school deal?"

"Three. But they're dealin' weight. Our gang will act as an enforcer."

"What's in it for the enforcers?"

"They get a little money or a share of the profits, kind of a stock interest. They will become virtual partners."

"So, they act as wholesalers for whites out in the county who, in turn, will sell it to their white customers?"

"Right."

"Any other gangs sell dope that way?"

"Yeah. The guys from Rose Terrace also sell only to whites. The gang from Oakdale . . . for them money is money. They sell to anyone." (The Rose Terrace Boyz was a group of about fifteen young men that was aligned with the Disciples. The Oakdales had approximately thirty members and were opponents of the Disciples and their various supporters.)

"Rose Terrace Boyz are a little smarter."

"How so?"

"Most of them have jobs, and they put their money in safety deposit boxes."

"For what are they saving?" I asked.

"I know three of them want to go to college. The Oakdales are stupid. As soon as they get some money, they get a car. That's how you get eyeballed by a police officer. They also don't have outside income to give them cover."

"If one of the Disciples has a bad deal, will his friends come to his assistance?"

"No. It will be a one-on-one thing with the other guy. If Slobs (Bloods) or Vicelords interferes, then they'll step in."

"Are the Disciples smart with their money?"

"Some might say they're smart."

"How so?"

"They put their money up and they save. They keep everything so subtle that the parents don't even know."

"For what are they saving?"

"Some for college. For others just for the fun of it."

"They spend it?"

"Yes. But they don't spend it in so outrageous a way as Oakdales do."

"Do the guys view it as a career?"

"No. They see it as a way to get out. Most of these kids came from the projects anyway. So they see it as a way to get out."

"Most view it this way?"

"Basically. Except I'm not sure about the Kings though . . . twenty-eight thousand dollars a week, times fifty-two weeks. That's a lot of money."

I wanted to be certain that I had heard him correctly. "You mean the three high school guys dealing in weight each pull in about twenty-eight thousand a week?"

"Just about."

"Is that profit or does it cover their expenses, too?"

"That's how much one kid's stuff is worth. Each week they may put five thousand dollars away. The rest goes to buy more product or for other expenses. I know one who's stashed more than a half-million dollars."

"And the other two?"

"About two hundred-fifty thousand. But one of the three plans to get out of it. He plans on goin' to college and become a biologist."

"So this isn't a stupid kid, is he?"

"No."

"Let's say I'm that kid, and I go to the state university. Am I ever out of it?"

"In that case probably not."

"What do you mean by that?" I asked.

"I mean that you have to tie up all the loose ends of your life, and there's only one way when it comes down to gettin' out of the drug business."

"And what might that be?"

"Lose yourself. Got to forget where you lived at. Got to make sure nobody can find you. Going to the state university isn't goin' far enough."

"Surely his friends know what he plans to do?"

"No. One day you just don't show up."

"And he's told none of his friends?"

"No."

I weighed my next words carefully. "But clearly," I said, "he told you."

Tyrone's eyes jumped, but just barely. He said nothing for a long moment. I broke the silence with my next question.

"What will happen when he doesn't show up? What will his friends say?"

"Nothin'."

"So then he's out of it?"

"Not really. Once you're in, you're in it for life."

"Can any demands be put on you in your new home?"

"None."

"Do you return on holidays?"

"You have enough money to live wherever you want. You might say you're set for the rest of your life, just about."

"What do my parents say when I don't come home?" I inquired.

Again Tyrone paused before answering. "Leave them a little note. Let 'em know what's goin' on. Leave them what's in a bank account, and that's the end of the discussion."

"And they'll accept that?"

Tyrone dropped his eyes. "Hope so."

I decided to change the direction of our discussion for a moment. I asked, "Do kids who sell a lot of dope usually give their parents money while they're still dealing?"

Tyrone shook his head. "No, 'cause then the parents start figurin' out." He changed his voice to sound like that of a concerned adult and said, "Where you gettin' all this money from, son?"

"Does it happen often that parents ask their children for money?"

"No, 'cause those guys who are asked are the ones who are stupid. You're not supposed to sell out of the house you're livin' in. That's a 'no no.'"

"How do the people dealing in weight come to meet their customers who live way out in the county?"

Tyrone shrugged his shoulders a bit. "Out joyridin' one night and you just run into some 'space head.'"

"Space head?"

"A person who likes to do crack."

"And he becomes the retailer?"

"Uh hum."

"It must be risky to move that much product," I stated.

"Not really. Just expensive," Tyrone responded.

"What do you mean?"

"Well, some cops cooperate with gangs. One or two in a district."

"What do they do?"

"Nothin'. They don't see it. They don't hear it."

"What do the cops get in return?"

"Five thousand a week."

"How does it work?"

"It happens when that one cop's on duty."

"So the dealer knows when it's safe?"

"That's right. But the five grand also buys him information about what's goin' on inside the police department like when the shifts are comin' on and goin' off duty. That's a good time to move the stuff."

"Someone with that kind of information would have to be pretty high up in his gang," I suggested.

"The highest," replied Tyrone without hesitation.

"What happens when someone that big leaves the organization?"

"There's someone in line to take over."

"How do girls figure in all of this?"

"Girls?" he replied. "Some girls get in it just to be in it. They won't be hassled by male cops, so they'll carry for guys."

"Are these the so-called 'drug whores' everybody talks about?"

"Yes."

"What's their cut?"

"Whatever the guy decides. Typically, a thousand."

"What about little kids?"

"No little kids. That's one ethic I hold. I don't know about anybody else. I may give it to a sixth grader [to hold]. Other than that they won't get it from me. They should be sixteen or older before you use them as holders or runners, but some guys use younger ones."

"Is that how a kid makes himself available to become a gang member?"

"No. It's like you have to prove yourself in a big fight. A recruiter has to see you. Then he tells me, and I say I'll think about it."

"If you approve, then what happens?"

"Two Violators will fight the wannabe. If he pass, he's in."

"And what does that get him?"

"A one-way trip to nowhere. But I made my mistake."

"What mistake was that?"

"Comin' into this big mess."

"Do other persons know that you regret it?"

"No, 'cause I hide my emotions so well. But when you find out you're losin' your heart, it's all over."

"You going to pull up stakes and leave your parents that letter?"

"Uhm hum. They'll find out what's goin' on when I leave 'em my checkin' account . . . I'll take what's in my safety deposit box and head south."

"How much are you going to take with you?"

"Like I told you . . . one has up to a half."

"And in the account?"

"Fourteen thousand."

"Will he send them anything else after a while?"

"Probably send them a letter. Tell them how he's doin'."

"So the kid's buying himself a new life," I stated.

"You might say."

"Scared?"

"Not really."

"Anxious?"

"Yeah. Ready to get out. Already got my acceptance letter."

"Any regrets?"

"Yes. I've seen a lot of people get hurt."

"Badly?"

"Badly. One guy lost his girl friend. He regrets that."

"What happened? She get caught in the middle?"

"Naw. She found out what he was doin'. He wanted to . . . tell her the truth, but she couldn't deal with it. If he hadn't been in this mess, he probably would have had a date for the prom. Who knows."

"Any other kind of hurt?"

"Once we seen one guy and girl get it . . ."

"That's when you decided it was a short-term proposition?"

"We already knew it wasn't goin' to be long term. Once we found out we could probably get accepted into almost any college that we wanted, that's when we just said 'Awright!' Asked our parents. They say, 'We don't have the money.' Went out. Got the money our own self."

"Would you have gotten into this stuff, if your parents had said they could help you?"

"Maybe. Maybe not. It's a lot of money."

"You ever been in trouble at school?"

"Only once. Got a one-day suspension . . . 'Cuz like I say, you can do anything, if you're an angel."

"And you're an angel?"

"All the teachers up here think so. Only five kids know what I really am." He cocked his head to the left. "That's one of my boys out there." He was referring to the young man sitting on the bench.

I nodded. "You going to make it?" I asked.

He pursed his lips a bit, then said, "Yeah. I'm goin' to make it."

I turned off my recorder and thanked him for talking with me. He said, "You're welcome." Then he turned and walked out of the room. If he said or did anything to communicate with his confederate, I did not see it. At least his friend seemed not to acknowledge any cue as Tyrone walked past him.

I motioned to him to join me, and he walked down the corridor to the conference room. There was a swagger in his walk that Tyrone had not shown. "This ought to be interesting," I said to myself.

The young man took the same seat that his friend had sat in and listened to the same speech I had made over four hundred times, most recently to Tyrone. He asked no questions. I began my interview.

"Do you know anything about gangs in the Fairview School District?"

"No."

"How about drug dealing?"

"Nope."

"Well, I'm going to read to you the names of some gangs from the area, and I'd like you to tell me if you've heard of any of them." I read part of the list and made sure that I included the name of his gang on it.

"Heard of any of them?"

He shook his head.

I stared at him for a moment. He returned my stare.

"Okay," I said. "Thanks for your help. You can go back to your class now."

He nodded even as he was rising from his seat. I did not watch him leave the room, because I was already packing my materials and recorder into my briefcase. I left the room as unceremoniously as he had. When I passed the Principal's office I stopped for a moment by his secretary's desk. Smiling, I said, "Please thank Mr Turner for all of his help. Yours too. I'm finished."

"You won't be back tomorrow?"

"No ma'am. That won't be necessary. Thanks again for all your help." I turned and walked out of the school for the last time. As I noted earlier, you know that you have talked to enough persons when there are no new stories to get.

I had acquired many good stories in the eight months that I spent interviewing students in the Fairview School District. Tyrone Jones's story was only the last but by no means the only poignant one I heard. It was exceptional only for the amounts of money involved in his drug dealing and because it tapped so many ideas expressed in bits and pieces by the hundreds of students who had preceded him.

Tyrone had pushed poison, hurt many persons, and amassed a great deal of money in the space of a few years. He also was finding it difficult to face the reality of what he had done and what he had become. I suspected that he was going to have more difficulty "making it" in the conventional world than his words had indicated. I also believed that somewhere behind those tired eyes Tyrone already knew this.

The younger man who followed Tyrone into the conference room, one of Tyrone's "boys," had not yet learned the lessons Tyrone had learned. There was still too much puff and strutter in his gait. I imagined that Tyrone might have walked that way once, but did not really believe it.

Tyrone's disclosures revealed a great deal about the making and unmaking of a gang member. It spoke to certain common features in the lives of young black men and women, and other persons from similar circumstances, for whom "ganging" is a reasonable expression of sociability and a way to acquire a measure of security. At the same time, his conversation revealed the tentative and brittle character of the social bonds developed in many gangs and the limits imposed on the personal freedom or financial security achieved through them. Tyrone's personal history illustrates well those ideas and features about gangs that draw young persons to such groups but can also drive them away.

The experiences of Tyrone and other young persons with whom I spoke were compelling, but they may not be universal. It is important to keep in mind that these children and students did not live in the deteriorated slums of some inner city or attend schools that were collapsing around them. They lived in nearly two dozen municipalities located on the perimeter of a city. They attended school in buildings that may have lacked some modern amenities, but they were a far cry from buildings that look like coiled snakes and blockhouses.

Both the towns in which they lived and the schools where they got an education had their problems, of course. Located in what social scientists call the "inner ring of suburbs" that surround cities, the towns comprising the Fairview School District underwent marked changes during the 1970s and 1980s. They may now vary in size quite a bit, but until the late 1960s the population of these towns had been overwhelmingly white. That changed as black families, many of them middle class, began their own exodus from a city to which tens of thousands of black people from the South had moved during and immediately after the Second World War. These were followed in the late 1970s and throughout the 1980s by increasing numbers of less well-to-do black families, some of which included only one adult. While these people were moving in, many white families were moving out to some of the very suburbs where Tyrone Jones's cocaine now was being sold by a white "space head."

Over the course of the 1980s, black persons had come to constitute nearly 70 percent of the population in these towns. Though there still was a substantial black and white middle-class element among the 41,000 persons living in these communities, increasing numbers of the less well-to-do have lowered the area's social and economic profile. The impact of these changes could be seen on the street, in the shops, and, perhaps most vividly, in the public schools.

Although there are over 1,500 white children between the ages of five and seventeen living in communities served by the Fairview School District, today the district educates fewer than 300 of them in its eleven schools. "Minority" students constitute over 90 percent of the district's student body of more than 5,000 youngsters.

More than three-quarters of the white children enrolled in the public schools attend elementary schools. Many white parents who kept their children in the elementary schools, either out of a sense of loyalty or because they could not afford the tuition of private and parochial schools, removed their children once they reached junior high school age. I saw many white and black children walking to local parochial schools in their uniforms or waiting for cars and buses that take them to some other private school.

Political and financial support for the public schools has diminished along with the size of their student body. A new superintendent, the district's first black chief administrator, found a dispirited staff and an accounting system badly in need of revision and closer supervision. He and his administrative staff made progress in both areas, sometimes with the cooperation of the school board and sometimes without it.

One of the problems that the new superintendent had found most troubling about his schools was the amount of fighting between youngsters from different towns. The fighting began in some elementary schools and peaked at the junior high school. There was less of it at the high school. Yet several particularly nasty exchanges at school-sponsored athletic events and dances, and a well-publicized visit to the high school by police officers with dogs trained to sniff out caches of drugs, had convinced him that something more serious than town rivalries was taking place in his schools. Several principals told him that gangs were involved, and he believed them.

I first met the superintendent, Bruce Sawyer, at a small meeting involving county and local officials who feared that gangs were beginning to have an impact on communities outside of the city. Bruce listened intently to my brief presentation about work that I had done in the city and asked me to visit his district. It was there that he, I, and the Director of Pupil Services, David Hoffman, had the first of many meetings regarding what was to become a study of gangs in the Fairview School District.

None of us knew what I would discover or how I would be received. We were well aware of the risks involved. Something truly awful might be uncovered. Students might take offense at my questions. A parent or outraged school board member might make a big public stink over the project. We knew that not all of the school principals were enthusiastic about the project. Several expressed their conviction that gangs were not a problem in their schools. Others were equally convinced that they were.

David, who is white, and Bruce, decided to go ahead with the project. They did so despite the reservations of some administrators and the real risk to their jobs should anything nasty take place as a result of my work. That took courage. Just for the record, we never heard one complaint about the interviews.

It also took courage, or at least a whole lot of faith, for young persons like Tyrone Jones to speak with me. I have some sense of why they felt confident enough to share as much with me as they did. Part of it might be that they heard that I had not divulged what they said to school authorities. In matters involving gangs and drug dealing one's reputation can make a great deal of difference. Certainly the promises that I made to them had an impact; but promises are not necessarily worth much in this line of work. It is just as likely that sensitive pieces of information fed to me from time to time that did not find their way to the principal or police helped more. I suspected that the most important reason they were willing to talk with me was rather more straightforward. I was an adult who was willing to listen and to take seriously, though not uncritically, what they said about something important to them. On the other hand, the youngsters simply might have thought that I was harmless and a diversion from their daily routine. In truth, any or all of these explanations might help to account for the reception most students gave me.

They wanted to talk about this part of their lives. They liked the idea, as I had presented it on numerous occasions, that they were to teach me. I was the student. It just so happened that I asked questions that they could answer with authority.

No matter how much they might have wanted to talk or how much faith they dared to invest in me, they often remained tentative and guarded. Many had good reason to behave that way. They did not all come to trust me during our conversation, and those like Tyrone who did came to it only gradually. They talked with me nonetheless. On the pages that follow, I will relate what they taught me about gangs and being a gang member.

Notes

1 Martin Sanchez Jankowski wrote an award-winning book entitled *Islands in the Street* (Berkeley, Calif.: University of California Press, 1991) which is described on the dust jacket as "a daring and hard-hitting examination of urban gangs." In my opinion it is an ethical travesty and testimony to the social scientist's ability to fool himself. Sanchez not only studied gangs in several cities, but he was initiated into them as well. He lived closely with them, fought in some of their fights, and witnessed crimes that were purposely staged to test whether he would turn in his would-be confederates. The results of his work did not take us much further in our understanding of gangs, and, again in my opinion, he badly misinterpreted some of what he saw. His ability to become physically close to gang members did not guarantee him access to information or a finer appreciation of the behavior he witnessed.

2 There were 5,664 students in the Fairview School District the year I did my work there. Approximately 400 of them agreed to speak with me. This represented about 7 percent

of the entire student population. I met with girls and boys, young women and men, in each school. More males than females were interviewed, and more black students than white students met with me. This was not inappropriate inasmuch as boys were more likely to engage in gang activity and the student population as a whole was more than 94 percent black.

I interviewed about two dozen students in each of the eight elementary schools that I visited. These 200 boys and girls constituted 6 percent of the elementary school population. At least 100 students were interviewed in both the junior and senior high school. This represented 11.5 percent of the junior high school population and over 6.5 percent of the high school's student body. Gang membership and activity was most pronounced in the junior high school. That was why a larger portion of its student population ended up being interviewed. If one considers that the target population of my study really did not include any students younger than ten years of age, then I probably interviewed at least 10 percent of the relevant student population.

3 Each elementary school principal considered between 5 and 10 percent of the students informed on such matters. The junior high school principal thought that less than 3 percent of his 868 students were knowledgeable. The senior high school principal provided a list that included only 1.5 percent of the 1,500 students enrolled in his school.

2

Gangs in the World of Children

Gangs and Gang Members

If I had asked a number of adults in the 1960s what they thought a gang is, my guess is that they would have come up with a pretty serviceable definition. Their conception of gangs might not have been as elegant or analytically sharp as a definition offered by someone who worked with gangs or studied them, but I doubt that it would have struck me as silly or groundless. What probably would have come to mind is a small group of teenage males born into one or another of America's less reputable ethnic groups, who lived in a slum, felt some odd attachment to the place, hung around with each other, and engaged in delinquent acts from time to time. Embedded in this definition of gangs was a clear notion of who belonged to these groups. The members were boys or young men who lived in inner-city neighborhoods with little money and even less social status.

If I were to ask a comparable number of adults today what they thought a gang was, my guess is that much of the "old" definition would hold up. Gangs still would be seen as a phenomenon of poor inner-city neighborhoods populated by members of a minority population. Young males would have remained the most likely candidates for membership; but more attentive observers would note that young females also were known to form gangs today. There might be some acknowledgment that gangs still serve an important social function for their members. Much more attention, however, would be placed on the terrible violence inflicted by gang members upon each other and upon innocent citizens. Our hypothetical group of surveyed adults also would speak at great length about the involvement of contemporary gang members in the sale of illegal narcotics and drugs.

It is likely that the conventional wisdom about gangs in the 1960s had at least a few holes in it. Gangs probably were more varied and complex than was commonly understood at the time. We should entertain the possibility that our view of contemporary gangs will someday be treated with equal skepticism by a new generation of clear-eyed observers.

The character of gangs no doubt has changed in important ways, and with it our understanding of what gangs are and who is likely to belong to these groups probably ought to change. These are topics that I will explore throughout this book. Right now I want only to note that however much a misleading caricature our portrayal of gangs and gang members may be, it has the advantage of having been filtered through many sources of information and perhaps some reflection on personal experience as well. When one talks to young children about gangs, as I did for the material in this chapter, it is important to bear in mind that they have no sense of history, comparatively few sources of information, and only limited experience to bring to the discussion. Whatever they know about gangs, or think they know, has been drawn largely from television or movies and a small circle of acquaintances, compressed into a short span of time, and embellished by a vivid imagination.

I cannot say with any certainty when children first became aware of gangs or what peculiar set of circumstances brought gangs to their attention. Until they reached the age of nine or ten, however, most children I interviewed had only the slightest idea of what a gang was, much less that gangs held a rather prominent spot on the fringes of the world they inhabited. After the age of eleven, or about the time they entered the fifth or sixth grade, all that apparently changed. Children began to speak about gangs in their towns and to relate stories about their peers practicing to become gang members. The existence of gangs became a commonly accepted fact for a large number of children, if not a universally shared experience, and ideas about gangs rushed at them from a variety of sources.

Among the children I interviewed there still were some fifth and sixth graders who remained largely ignorant of gangs except for what they learned through the media and their conversations with friends. Gang activity was not so pervasive a phenomenon that all children found it impossible to avoid. Nevertheless, virtually all children by this age had heard of gangs and had begun to make some sense of what gangs were and who belonged to them. Gangs were something that a lot of children wanted to learn more about and spent some time discussing among themselves. Their knowledge of gangs, however, remained suspect.

I asked children to name gangs with which they were familiar. Many were able to identify a few such groups, but it was rare that someone named more than three or four gangs. Some named gangs that came from the city. Other children named gangs that apparently did not exist. One of these groups, the Fairview Girlz, was identified by some children as being in the high school. A few children even made brief references to the exploits of its members. When I inquired about this group in my conversations with students at the high school, however, no one had heard of it. The Fairview Girlz was the idealized prototype of a gang to which some children had attributed traits that gangs were supposed to possess.

When I asked children to tell me which gangs "got along well" and which ones "were fighting," they were able to construct a picture that portrayed gangs being aligned in two broad coalitions. They all knew that Crips and Bloods were opponents and stood at the top of these coalitions, but they offered no reason why the Los Angeles gangs should hold such a lofty position. In these pictures, children also were able to arrange under the Crips and Bloods a number of the local gangs that were found in the towns served by the Fairview School District. Their sense of which local gangs were aligned with these much larger organizations when compared to information shared by older students and knowledgeable adults, however, was rather poor. They tended to put several of the bigger and more active gangs in the Fairview School District in the wrong coalition. This was rather like placing professional baseball or football teams in the wrong division, except that in this case an error could have serious consequences for anyone venturing into the "wrong" town or saying publicly which gangs he favored.

A good number of children were able to identify accurately those gangs present in the Fairview School District. A few children also could place some of these gangs in the correct coalition, but most children could not. I do not think that the children were misrepresenting what they knew, or thought they knew. They had only limited familiarity with gangs in their own towns and even less information about gangs in other communities.

Most of us who chronicle what people do and say would not worry too long about events that do not occur. We want to be where the action is, not where the action isn't. Many children in the Fairview School District were not aware of much gang activity. If they were right, then there would have to be more promising places to study gangs. We probably would be better off paying more attention to some inner-city neighborhood, and that is precisely what most reporters, researchers, and self-appointed crusaders do when it comes to working with gangs or trying to figure them out. After all, who is likely to read or listen well to what we say about gangs and, not coincidentally, fund our special program or research project on the subject when most of our prospective clients seem immune to the difficulties we propose to address, or at least study?

I believe, nonetheless, that there is good reason to take seriously the apparent inability of many younger children to recognize that gangs might be operating around them. There could be many explanations for this phenomenon, including the ability of parents to shield their children from the presence and effect of gangs. Gangs also may not have been as important as some children thought and more adults feared. Existing gangs may have been so small, tame, or geographically isolated as to render them invisible to all but those individuals in the immediate area. Alternatively, gangs may not have stood out in the minds of many children precisely because these groups were not an exceptional feature in the community. Gangs may have been all over the place but not construed as an alien presence worthy of special attention. They may have fitted more readily in these communities than popular prejudice or some "scientific" theories would have one predict. Furthermore, this might be no less true even though gang members sometimes behaved in ways that provoked fear and harsh criticism from many quarters.

The inability of many children to identify with any appreciable accuracy the gangs in their own neighborhoods and surrounding communities posed an interesting problem. At the same time they were going to and from school or venturing out to play, individuals not much older than themselves were roaming the streets, menacing at least some children, and carrying out a variety of crimes. It occurred to me that one reason that children might not have been sufficiently alert to the activities of gangs was that gangs or groups we chose to call "gangs" were not an exceptional feature in the community. Much of what children said about gangs and gang members led me to believe this was the case.

Gangs were not at all uncommon in the towns served by the Fairview School District. Sprinkled throughout many of my conversations with children were observations like the following:

"I got in one last year. We weren't bad. We got together to try to get money to buy candy and stuff."

"Is that a gang?"

"Not exactly. There were ten of us. Everybody had money at their house, and they brought a quarter a week. Or they can bring fifty cents and pay for two weeks." He began to laugh, then added, "That didn't last too long."

"Run out of quarters?"

"Yeah."

Another youngster related a similar story about how his groups of friends managed to acquire and share relatively expensive video game cartridges. They took odd jobs or parts of their allowances and contributed a sum of money to a common fund. Tapes were purchased with this money, and the cartridges were circulated among the members of the group. The young man telling the story indicated that he was allowed to use the tapes first, because he had organized the enterprise.

Still other children spoke of groups that certainly struck them as being more like a real gang.

"They're around," one boy said. "I see them . . . wear a lot of blue and red. Wear a blue rag in their back pocket."

"They're all around here," another indicated. "Everywhere. In my whole neighborhood they sell drugs."

A girl stated the she knew "there are gangs in [her] neighborhood on the block behind [her]. The policeman told us."

Several other children made the following comments.

"Pine Ridge not really a gang. Just a group of boys thinking about becoming a gang."

"Milldale and Oakdale used to be close, but a lot of 'he-say she-say' stuff started fights between 'em a couple of years ago." By this they meant that two young men or women had exchanged unflattering remarks about each other, their friends, or family members.

"The kids from Banister say they sell drugs."

"That group be comin' around and shootin' and stuff. I saw a fight. The Vista Village fight the Milldale. The Milldale fight the Riveredge. One from Milldale sells drugs in my neighborhood. I turn around and walk the other way . . . when I see him."

"The 'V Boyz' [Vista Village Boyz] be comin' down to the store. They be crowdin' around my grandma's store, and the police come and tell 'em to move away."

"I know the Riveredge fight a lot up at the high school, like during basketball games. The next day they'll line up across each other on Maple Street and walk off somewhere and start fightin.'"

Finally, there was this exchange that I had with a big, tough-looking thirteen-year-old from a town that had a well-known gang.

"You're telling me," I said incredulously, "that you've lived there for thirteen years and never heard of the Riveredge Posse?"

"No."

"Ever heard of Santa Claus?"

"Yes."

"What about the Easter Bunny?"

"Yup."

"How about the 'V Boyz'?" (an avowed enemy of the Riveredge Posse).

"Yes."

"But you've not heard of the Riveredge Posse?"

"No."

It was apparent from many comments like these that numerous children had an awareness of gangs or something they took to be a gang. They also were not oblivious to the real or imagined dangers of being involved with gangs. As one boy put it, "We were playing around. Pretending we were

like from LA. Sometimes we wore blue. Sometimes we wore red. But we
stopped . . . two years ago."

"Why?"

"There were gangs out here. Young kids are dyin' 'cause of gangs and
drugs. So I just stopped."

"What about your friends?"

"I got them to stop. Told 'em we'd better stop hangin' 'round like we
some gang members. Have to start playin' somethin' else."

Many children held similar views of gangs. Indeed, a number of them
believed that death or the threat of dying was central to much of gang life.
Thus, when I asked a boy how someone became a gang member, he
answered without hesitation that you "have to kill somebody." I received
a similar response from another child when I asked what happened if a drug
deal went badly. He thought that his fellow gang members would kill him
for losing the group's "product." Other youngsters spoke of being killed
in the context of drug deals or gang fights, but at the hands of his customers
or enemies.

The idea of killing someone or being killed also came up routinely in
discussions about ending one's gang affiliation. One boy noted that "if you
a Crip," and want to get out, you "got to kill a Blood." A second boy
said that to sever one's ties with the Disciples, Tyrone's gang, "you got
to kill your mother." Another youngster noted that one had to kill either
his mother or his father, if he wanted to leave a particular local gang. When
I asked him if he had ever known this to happen, he shook his head. He
quickly added that one's only option under those circumstances was to be
killed himself. He had heard of one boy who was so badly hounded that
his family had to leave town in order to protect him.

The individuals involved in these stories were not known to the children
relating the tale. This added a sense of mystery and foreboding to each related
event. Only once was a specific child identified as the alleged killer, and
it happened that he had moved only recently into the area from another state.
There was much speculation about him. Students were certain that his family
had been forced to leave their former home because the boy had committed
a murder in order to leave his gang. We were assured that even the "tough
kids" at the school left this boy alone. I was not especially surprised to learn
from the counselor that nothing in her records indicated anything out of
the ordinary about the transfer student's history.

For many children, then, gangs were mysterious, scary, and exciting all
at the same time. References to gangs often conveyed vivid images of
physical danger and fear of the unknown. Particularly relevant in this regard
were stories told about gangs and a local cemetery. It seems that the
graveyard was a spot that real or aspiring gang members frequented.

The cemetery, as one child put it, was where the members of one gang count their drug money and just hang out." A second youngster told how "at nighttime in the graveyard . . . they be down there shootin.'" Other children tied the cemetery to initiation rites practiced by several gangs. As one boy said, "Ya gotta walk through the cemetery at night" to become a member. Another indicated that his friends had said prospective members must sleep in the graveyard all night, if they wanted to join a gang.

What emerged from my discussions with children was a picture of gangs that combined elements of play and dreadful seriousness. The play and camaraderie evident in gangs were reminiscent of the adventurous "Lost Boys" on Peter Pan's island called Neverland. There among the six living members of that band was Slightly, "the most conceited of the boys . . . [who] thinks he remembers the days before he was lost, with their manners and customs."[1] The danger and depravity in gangs was for children, expresses in their view of gangs as groups that had abandoned or rejected the manners and customs of a more conventional adult world. Such a group had much more in common with the rampaging tribe of youngsters portrayed in *Lord of the Flies*. It was another collection of "lost boys" who murdered and destroyed symbols of their civilized selves so that there was no one any longer "to talk sense" or any "solemn assembly for debate . . . [and] dignity" remaining.[2]

Children managed to create a coherent view of gangs that combined elements of a band of "lost boys" on holiday and a rampaging tribe capable of terrible acts. They had to work hard to do so, because their impressions and contacts with groups called "gangs" and persons calling themselves "gang members" came at them in a sudden rush. They labored to determine more precisely where they stood, or wanted to stand, in relation to gangs and gang members. It made no difference to the children that some of them had little or no exposure to gangs. It mattered only that they were able to construct explanations about gangs that made sense to them. So it was that one boy quite frightened by gangs could say "most of these gang members ran away . . . from home. They travel all around places. Hang around and hurtin' people." They, too, it seems, were lost boys.

Trying on the Gang Role

The boy who spoke of gang members as runaways or discarded children was one of many who observed gangs and, less frequently, served as targets of their petty tyrannies. After I completed my interview with him, he asked me in a rather sad voice if I might catch these boys and put them in jail. I gently reminded him that my job was to study what gangs were doing and that I could not arrest these boys no matter how nasty they were. He seemed more resigned than disappointed. I asked him why he wanted them put in jail. He looked at me and the school counselor and said, " 'Cause I'd really like to go outside and play. But I can't really go out alone in the back yard, 'cause they be runnin' around shootin'."

"Your mom won't let you play in your backyard?"

"Not really. Unless I'm with a grown person."

"Where can you play?"

"My basement."

"Is that where you and your friends play?"

"Yes, unless I play on my porch."

"But you know that can be dangerous sometimes, don't you?"

He nodded his head. I had realized at some point in our conversation that another child had told us a story about a boy who, along with a friend, had been chased to his front porch by some "gang members'" from the neighborhood. The two friends had beaten frantically on the front door until the first boy's mother came out and chased the gang from the porch.

This youngster was not alone in expressing his fear about gangs he had observed. Other children, too, had been confined to their house after school, had tried to avoid gangs by taking different routes home, or had been instructed by their parents not to visit certain places known to be frequented by gang members. Most children were not cloaked from the influence of gangs to such an extraordinary degree. On the other hand, some were quite anxious about coming upon a group of such youngsters loitering on the street, playing in a park, or simply standing on a school playground during recess. They took different steps to avoid being harassed, and much of the time they appeared to have been successful.

Another collection of youngsters was not at all anxious about gangs. These children took no steps to guard themselves from being exposed to gangs or gang members. Indeed, they experimented in a casual way with something they called "gangs." For many of these children, fighting either one other person or in a larger group was an important way for them to "try on" the persona of a gang member and to see how agreeable it was to them.

"How are new members selected for that gang?" I inquired of one boy.

"They'll pick a person [who's] got a reputation for fighting a number of guys at once. You're tough. They'll talk and invite you. If you say no, they may beat you up. If you say yes, they'll ask you to help them."

On other occasions, the youngster wishing to become more involved may make his interests known to older boys. "They know people in the junior high and senior high. They ask them how they can get in the group." If they are accepted, these younger boys "go around with [the gang members] and help them fight." The number of opportunities to be observed or to make oneself available was pretty large. Youngsters from different towns were fighting on a regular basis. One group would purposely encroach upon the "territory" of a second group and fight its resident gang members. This provoked subsequent incursions into their town by the gang whose territory had been violated.

The fights settled nothing, but this does not mean that they were insignificant. Their importance came from the fact that they expressed in muscular terms a respect and pride for the town in which the combatants lived. Communal brawls like these are well represented in the history of Europe and the United States. They always have done more to reaffirm the loyalty of persons to their town or village than to resolve any real or putative grievance between them and the inhabitants of the next town over.

Communal brawls in some form or other had occurred in the Fairview School District for a long time, teachers had reported. There was nothing novel about the reasons for fighting that black youth espoused. I only was certain that there would be other incursions on other days. Nothing much would come of them either, especially since the territory that was violated was in no danger of being taken in any permanent way by persons from another township.

These conflicts were important for another reason. They often spilled over into the schools. Junior high school students seemed particularly eager to fight, in large measure because it was the first place that students from different towns had sustained exposure to each other. Fights also occurred outside of elementary schools at the end of a day when junior high school students from one town went looking for trouble at an elementary school located in an opponent's territory. Children at the elementary schools, however, also fought among themselves with some regularity.

Gangs instigated fights with individuals just passing through their town. Such attacks did not need to be provoked by a specific challenge coming from a recognized opponent. As one youngster said, "If they don't know some people ... they'll just fight ... to show what they represent."

"To show that they're tough?" I asked.

"Yes." He also noted, however, that it was the group incursions that led to the largest fights. "They'll go round up a lot of dudes. You know they got their cousins. They get bigger by gettin' their cousins and their cousin's friends, and they keep growin'."

"What will they use in a fight?"

"They come at you with chains, guns, and stuff. Anything they have. It can happen any time they ready, too."

"Girls at this age also had become organized into groups. Though not as numerous or as large as the boy's gangs, the girls were active and fought quite a bit. I asked a girl how one became a member of the Milldale Girlz. She gave me a most incredulous look and said, in a tone that conveyed her disdain for my stupid question, "They live there."

"What do they do?"

"Go around beatin' up people."

"What kind of people?" (another stupid question).

"Girls!"

"Why?"

"Because some girls in Milldale are weak."

"What else do you do?"

"Just hang around at the shopping mall after school." (She might have added that girl gang members typically did a lot of shoplifting at the mall.)

"Do you ever fight girls from other groups?"

"Yes. They'll fight in alleys, streets, or in the playground. Mostly on weekends."

"Have you ever hurt somebody in one of those fights?"

"Yes. Probably broke their nose."

Because of what girls told me it seems plausible to suggest that their fights were not as numerous, large, or violent as the fights mounted by boy gangs. It was rare that they fought alongside boy gangs. A more likely occurrence was for them to try to stop the boys from fighting, " 'cause when the boys pull out guns . . . the girls get all frightened and stuff. She be tryin' to hold him back . . . try to take the guns from 'em. Maybe two or three of them try to do this to the main guy, the girls call 'the master.' "

"He has three girls? What does he do with them?"

"I don't know. He'll be kissin' 'em. He just messes around with 'em and stuff."

These occasional attempts by girls to take the boys' minds off fighting illustrate an important feature of gang life for youngsters at this age. Not everyone affiliated with gangs is totally committed to all of the gang's adventures. A number of boys also try to limit their involvement and actually back away from the possibility of gang membership at this point. As one boy put it, "Things were getting too rough."

One boy acknowledged that he had been a Junior Disciple. He had participated in a few fights and was learning more of the signs that enabled one to challenge, insult, and/or communicate with opponents and allies. However, he had yet to earn any "credits" by shooting someone or committing other specified tasks. He decided to drop out after one fight in which someone shot at him. The bullet hit a gate as he ran through it.

Other boys related similar stories about leaving their respective gangs. One in particular spoke rather clearly about his reasons for quitting and the impact of severe fights on individual members and the gang as a whole. "I was in it about two years. Went in at ten."

"Why did you get out?"

"They had too many fights. I didn't want to go where they go."

"Where was that?"

"Sometimes they like go to the skating rink and do shootin'. They sell marijuana. I say I don't want no part of that. Some quit. I quit. Membership went down . . . [and] the gang paid kids to help them fight when their numbers are low. It happened two times. Once when the guy we hired did an especially good job he was paid extra. One kid was shot in . . . the leg in that fight."

"Who took care of him?"

"The gang members."

"What did they do?"

"They just tried to get the thing out" [at their homes].

"You dug it out?"

"Um hm. That's what they be doin'. Sometimes they tell their mothers they got cut and stuff."

"Does the parent believe them?"

"No. Sometimes they call the police up to their house."

I spoke to another boy from a different town who told a similar story. He went into more graphic detail about the surgical procedures employed than did the youngster whom I just quoted. He spoke of how they probed around the entry point and cauterized the wound after the bullet had been removed. The event had impressed this second boy and his friends.

The collection of youngsters who tried on a gang identity put themselves in places where gang members were found and attempted to act like the gang members they saw. They took a few steps toward making themselves into gang members and took some satisfaction from brief tastes of a "gang life." It was not hard to go this far, because they often knew quite well the youngsters involved in "gang activities." In their own minds, however, they had not yet made a full commitment to becoming a gang member. They did not see themselves as novitiates.

Other children and older, more established members of local gangs probably saw them as probationary members of such groups. However marginal their involvement and half-hearted their commitment, children who experimented with a gang identity would have been hard to distinguish from those more serious about gangs. They lived on the same blocks, played and went to school together, conspired as all children do to act older than they were, and did many things together as a group. Gangs emerged quite naturally from such circumstances. It is possible and even likely that those children who experimented with being a gang member and then curtailed their involvement could still be counted on in a fight against youngsters not from their group, gang, or community.

It is to the youngsters who experiment with gangs and those who actually become novitiates that the term "wannabe" ordinarily is applied. Tyrone Jones had spoken more broadly of wannabes as anyone who had not passed a rather involved and lengthy period of testing. More individuals called themselves Disciples than had been formally "made," or initiated. Yet his gang was based in Chicago. The criteria one needed to satisfy in order to become a full-fledged member in a local gang were looser. It may have been just as important in local gangs to prove oneself or show that one had "heart," but one's experience as a probationary member was shorter, filled with fewer tests, and taken more casually. Established gang members already had a good sense of the kind of person their home-grown wannabe was.

Children who were serious prospects for gang membership distinguished themselves by their willingness to fight more and to use weapons – or at least carry them. They also became involved in criminal activities on a routine basis. Those children I have referred to as "experimenters" might have been involved in one or another illegal activity from time to time, but they stood on the margins of whatever schemes to make money were being plotted. The serious wannabe was among the plotters and prime executors of these schemes.

Children recognized a certain gradation in the crimes they and their peers committed. Among the least serious offenses to them were petty extortion and robbery. Boys and girls affiliated with gangs spoke openly about taking money or personal items from other children. The items included everything from candy to clothing. Sometimes the victims gave up the money or item in return for the promise that they would not be molested. On other occasions they were pushed, hit, or kicked until the money or item was relinquished. Unlike the situation in other communities, no one had yet been killed for these items in the towns comprising the Fairview School District. The process whereby such extortion or robbery took place was called "punking" and the victim was referred to as a "punk." A punk also was someone who refused to fight in the face of a challenge thrown down by another person. To call someone a punk was intended to be a serious insult, and most youngsters treated it that way.

Next on the list of popular crimes came burglary and shoplifting. Boys committed most of the burglaries and girls were primarily responsible for shoplifting. Houses and automobiles could be broken into without much difficulty or risk. Shoplifting appeared to be no harder. The value and variety of goods acquired through these activities were quite variable. Several youngsters indicated that with few exceptions it was the practice to commit such crimes outside one's home territory. The preferred location to carry out a home invasion or car burglary was the territory of an opposing gang. Youngsters spoke of "raiding parties" being mounted against gangs whose members had been pilfering items from their community.

The assistance of older boys, usually in their early teens, was helpful in committing car robberies and dealing drugs, but it was not required. These activities were more serious, in any case, because of the sums of money and levels of danger involved, the coordination necessary to carry out the crime, and the extensive contacts that individuals needed before the product could be "moved." These crimes also gained the most recognition from older and better established gang members.

Boys were introduced to these activities gradually. At first they would "go along for the ride" when cars were stolen, or they served as carriers and couriers during drug sales. A stolen car might bring them several hundred dollars which was split unevenly among those boys in attendance. The youngest children might receive twenty or thirty dollars for an afternoon or evening's work. Children who acted as couriers between the drug dealer and buyer could expect to make comparable sums but for less work than was entailed in stealing cars or stripping them of their more valuable parts.

Girls were especially prized as holders of drugs and beepers for the boys who dealt. I was told that unlike boys who were likely to run when approached by a police officer, girls usually stood their ground and even joked with the officer who had stopped them. Male officers are understandably reluctant to frisk females, and they often are prohibited from doing so by their department's regulations. Moreover, they did not like waiting for a female officer to come and assist them with a search. The boys shook their heads in admiration for the girls' sense of confidence. Several boys said the girls were really "cool" during these meetings.

Some boys who were less than thirteen years-old sold drugs, but comparatively few girls did. Those children who sold drugs were most likely to sell marijuana because it was cheap to acquire and easy to move. They occasionally sold a few pieces of crack cocaine, but it was simply too expensive to buy in any great quantity and difficult for children to sell. Competition was stiff, and they had less ability than did teenagers to search for new customers on the street.

The boys who sold drugs other than marijuana made a great deal of money for someone their age. One youngster knew of three boys at his school who sold crack. Two of them regularly came to school with two or three hundred dollars in their pockets. He told me that "they just started. They ask people in gangs who sell it. The people in gangs give 'em a hand with sellin', then the new sellers pay them back." The object of the younger boys was to go out on their own as soon as possible and not have to buy drugs from a primary source in a gang who made a tidy profit from such sales. The boys realized that they could make more money that way, but had not yet learned that going out on one's own also incurred much greater risks.

This early introduction of boys and girls to the metropolitan area's hidden economy held great appeal for a number of youngsters. It provided them with money that they "flashed" in front of their peers and used to buy jewelry, clothes, and other "toys." A number of children commented that the boys and girls who got money and "things" from such enterprises were among the more popular youngsters in their school or neighborhood. "They dress up," one girl noted. "Have money all the time."

I was surprised to learn how children hid money and expensive items from their parents. They could not claim, as older youngsters could, that they held a legitimate job. Instead, they found ways of stashing goods and money in their own homes and the residences of friends. They would change into fancy clothes after leaving home and change back into their regular clothing upon their return from school. They spent money on food or entertainment. They rarely saved money except to buy a particular item from a store or more drugs for their customers.

A good portion of the items purchased from stores went to girls as "presents." One girl told me that "if she go with a gang member, he'll give her money. She don't have to work or nothin'."

"Would you be expected to give him anything in return?" I asked.

"No."

Teenage girls knew better. Nonetheless, it was not hard to figure out why such boys and girls were popular. They had more money than any child should possess, and they spent it lavishly. I found their popularity and spending habits all the easier to understand in the wake of reports from school staff that many children in the district qualified for publicly subsidized meals or came to school at times in clothing that was worn out or still damp after being washed the previous evening.

I do not mean to imply that all gang members were poor or turned to criminal activities in order to put clothes on their backs and food in their bellies. I met gang members who came from households where one or both parents were in residence and were able to pay their bills. More gang members probably came from homes where money was tight, and some children in gangs no doubt came from poor families. In neither of these latter cases, however, would this have distinguished them from many poor and working-class children who were not involved with gangs.

Family, Neighborhood, and Schools

The family situation of some children did make it easier for them to fall in with gangs. However, I do not want to ignore the significance of the gang in its own right as an organizing force for both legitimate play or free-time activities and crime. Its impact was greater than that of the typical peer group, team, or club. Gangs shaped much of what passed as a normal social life for children involved with them and had a perceptible effect on the routines of other youngsters who were not participants. Moreover, there was an explicit and strong connection between the local gangs and the towns in which they were found. Every local gang took the name of a township as part of its title. Even children with little or no contact with gangs or gang members often used the name of a town as a substitute for a gang's whole title. Children knew that a reference to the "Milldale" was really shorthand for a gang called the Milldale Boyz. More than a fictive brotherhood, gangs brought together family members and friends in a union whose identity was bound to a specific place, their town.

It was important that both the group and the place were treated as objects warranting respect and capable of integrating even younger children into a world of work. That displays of respect often accompanied violence and that the work was largely illegal do not diminish the truth of this observation. The fact that children not affiliated with gangs also fought and committed crimes which brought them money does not limit its truthfulness either. Gangs gave structure and meaning to many fights and delinquent acts. They may not have made children behave poorly, but they certainly increased the opportunities for poor behavior, magnified its effects, and encouraged it with symbolic and material incentives.

The world of gangs was organized around three main pillars in the child's life: his family, neighborhood, and school. Each played an important part in defining what a gang looked like, how it behaved, and the manner in which children related to it. The gang, in turn, became so important a force in organizing the lives of its members as well as persons lacking any affection for it that families, neighborhoods, and schools all were shaped by it.

Families helped to make gang members by what they did and failed to do with their children. I spoke with a number of children whose parents apparently made a considerable and successful effort to insulate them from the influence of gangs. Other parents appeared to have been less successful despite having talked about the dangers of gangs, guns, and drugs on a fairly regular basis. Some parents just laid out general warnings such as "not to mess with guns and to stay away from those big fights." A few parents resorted to making threats that usually were ignored. One child who lived with his grandparents reported that his grandmother said, "next time I'm with a gang, she'll call the police and I'll go to jail."

Both boys and girls were warned about gangs or encouraged not to join one. One girl related how her "momma told me I'd better stay away from those boys. They wanted me to go do somethin' crazy with 'em. Go into an old house." A second girl said her mother was "afraid to let me go anywhere, even around to my friend Andrea's house. She has to know I'm goin' to be back, a time to call her to let her know where I am. She's scared 'cause she's seen what they do. They beat my brother so bad his eye was swollen." She added that her cousins wanted to look for the boys who beat her brother. "I'm not sayin' that's good, but I'm not sayin' it's all bad either. 'Cause if you're goin' to hurt my family, they're goin' to hurt you."

The idea of coming to the defense of one's kin is similar to that employed by gang members when they speak of punishing another group that came after some of their friends. There is one notable difference. Gang members see such a response as entirely justifiable. They express no reluctance to use force under such circumstances and frankly view it as their right to do so. There is no clash between conventional standards and the rules that they follow.

In many instances, when the appropriateness of violence or other dangerous behavior is at issue, the families of gang members accepted the subordination of conventional standards to the standards practiced by gangs. Many youngsters said that parents made some attempt to wean a child from gangs. They try to "get him to leave it," one boy told me, "but they can't get him to leave it." Other parents were more accepting, even supportive of their child's gang involvement. One boy laughed when I suggested that he knew a lot about Crips because of his township connection. "Nah, it's my family connection." Both of his older brothers were Crips and one sold drugs.

A number of children had older brothers and cousins who were in gangs, and this had drawn them to gangs. Some had fathers who had been in gangs when they were young, and gang membership was viewed as something of a rite of passage into adulthood. Other parents simply treated it as a necessary hazard that had to be negotiated on the way to becoming an adult.

I asked one boy named John Baker if his parents knew that he was a Disciple. He answered in the following way. "They know I am, but they don't really expect me to go out and fight. 'Cause I mostly stay home and like clean up and play."

"Do they know that your older-brother is a Disciple?"

"Yes."

"What do they say about that?"

"They really don't say. But they say when you get on the street and somebody hurts you, don't come cryin' to us . . ."

"Do they try to get him to quit?"

"Yeah. But then he goes right back in it."

"Is it the same for other kids' parents?"

"Yeah. They don't want to see their kid die. The way gangs are goin' around here somebody's goin' to get shot or somethin'."

"Some parents keep their kids under pretty tight restrictions. What do you think about that?"

John considered his answer carefully. He brushed his blond hair to one side and looked at me with clear blue eyes. "It's kinda OK, because you want to be safe."

"Are kids scared?"

"Sometimes. And sometimes they aren't."

"How safe are you?"

"I'm a messenger. Our leader tells us who we're goin' to hit on. We put on our boots so we don't step on anything that will hurt our feet. I go tell [the other gang] when we're ready. And they got a messenger that tells us when they're ready. They keep me on the outside so that I don't get hurt. But sometimes when people are jumping on one person, I jump in on it."

"Is that all?"

"Yeah, but please don't tell the other kids I'm a Disciple. This town doesn't have many, and I'd get beat up."

"Of course I won't tell anyone, but don' t your parents worry when you go out at night for these fights?"

He seemed a bit taken aback by my question.

"No," he answered. " 'Cause I have to be home by nine o'clock to go to bed."

After John left the room, I turned and looked at the counselor. "Did you have any idea . . ." She was shaking her head "No" even before I finished my question.

I had a quite different experience in another elementary school.

Yancey Vardar was as richly brown as John Baker was white. He, like John, was in the fifth grade and not bashful at all about talking to us. Yet he was different from John and every other child who had openly acknowledged some gang involvement. While other boys bragged about their exploits or related events only after being cajoled into doing so, Yancey expressed no emotion with his voice and gave no sign with his face of being touched by any of my questions.

He sat calmly at the table. The fingers of his hands were neatly laced. He did not avoid my eyes as some children did when relating a story, but when I looked at him I had the feeling that something was missing. He alternately admitted to engaging in gang activities and distanced himself from them, but there was no doubt that he was an active participant. He talked about hurting persons with the same nonchalance as you or I would talk about taking out the garbage.

"There are seven Crips at this school," he said. "I fight only one kid."

"Is he a Blood?"

"No. He a perpetrator . . . someone who talks in a different way. They always thinks they bad; and when you tell them to come get you, they don't move. Big talkers."

"What do you do as a Crip?"

"They kick people's doors in. We did it once. He's a Crip from California and lives in my neighborhood. He sells cocaine. Other kids sell it, too. On the corner."

"Would you take drugs?"

"No."

"Why not?"

"Because it's stupid."

"What else do you do?"

"I fight Bloods outside of school."

"Anyone in your family know this?"

"My two older brothers are both Crips. One in California. One live in my house. He sells cocaine."

"Is that how he makes money?"

Yancey answered with a simple, "Uh huh."

"Do they save it or spend it?"

"They spend it. They try to buy cars and stuff."

We talked a while longer, but it was hard for me. It was not that he said anything particularly shocking. I had heard other youngsters describe their fights or drug dealing, and most of them expressed themselves in colorful language and at times with excitement in their voice. Not so for Yancey. He presented his sentences in a clipped and practiced way that I found unnerving. There was no light in this child, no feeling. He was cold, and he frightened me.

After Yancey left the office, I waited for a moment before speaking to the counselor. When I finally spoke I told her, "I'm going to say something that I've never said about anyone before."

"What's that?" she asked.

"If that child doesn't kill someone, it's because somebody will kill him first. He's a murder waiting to happen."

This was a strong statement, and I expected the counselor to take offense at my remark. Instead, she displayed no great surprise. "Interesting you should say that," she said as she pulled a file from her desk drawer. For the next minute or so she read me excerpts from Yancey's file. In addition to coming from a troubled family, he had developed a rather nasty habit over the past two years. He started shooting birds and other small animals with his air rifle. When he grew tired of killing these beasts with the small lead balls shot from his rifle, he turned his toy on other children. Yancey would shoot them in the ankle while standing behind them. Of late, he had raised his sights and now was shooting them in the thigh.

"Good God," I said. "He's practicing how to kill." He was indeed preparing himself, growing more accustomed to the idea of shooting someone with a gun. He really *was* a murder waiting to happen.

There was a world of difference between Yancey Varder and Tyrone Jones, the retiring Gangster Disciple. Tyrone would kill a person, but only if it were necessary. Despite all the pain he had made for himself and for others, Tyrone understood that one could lose something important in oneself. He had a sense that there were limits beyond which one dared not venture lest he lose his soul. Yancey was perverse to the bone, cunning, a truly dangerous person. He would end up killing someone because he liked it. Sooner or later someone else would realize that he had an interest in killing Yancey.

Most children involved with gangs were more conscious of the choices they were making than was John Baker, the blond haired, blue eyed wannabe, and far less indifferent to the consequences of their actions than was Yancey Vardar. Notwithstanding their differences, all these children had some ties to a family and some adult supervision or care. Even though many of them seemed to have much freedom to roam great distances and to come home as they pleased in the evening, they did not enjoy the greater unsupervised liberties allowed to junior high school students.

Some adults were said not to know that the children under their roof were involved with gangs. Some were reported to know and tried to discourage that involvement. Others allegedly knew but did little to stop it. A minority of the families apparently behaved in a fashion that encouraged children to take up with gangs and to do whatever gang members did. Although a number of children might have had family members who sold drugs, I came across only a few who referred to their parents as drug dealers.

My point is that boys and girls in each of these different family situations knew well the children who merely observed their activities or who flirted with gang attachments. They also knew that their family was different in some ways and similar in some ways to the families of these other children. Each of these families may have kept secrets from their neighbors, but they held few surprises. The knowledge they possessed was shared with family members, neighbors, and acquaintances. That was one reason why the boundary line between those parts of a child's world belonging to gangs and the parts not belonging to gangs was not well defined. The information they held and the experiences they shared made it difficult, if not impossible, to create and maintain such walls.

Insofar as there were walls at all, it was the children and young men and women in and out of gangs who built them. It happened that most of the walls they built coincided with the boundary lines of their townships and, at least for the younger children, their elementary schools. That is why neighborhoods and schools played such an important part in making the world of gangs more understandable to children.

"The V Boyz are like our protection group," one boy told me. "Some people from Milldale be tryin' to rob people's house (in our town) and the V Boyz be windin' up catchin' 'em and fighting and stuff. They beat 'em real bad, then let 'em go. They also watch out for the little kids. Make sure Milldale don't bother 'em."

"Does the V Boyz do anything in Milldale?"

"Break into houses. Steal and sell things."

"How violent do the fights become?"

"At night they come up here and fight and shoot."

"Have you known anyone to be shot during one of these fights?"

"No. When they're gettin' ready to do the shoot out, some of 'em will hide behind logs and stuff. In the playground they hide behind the barrels and shoot [over the top without looking]. Then they'll peek their head around and see if the other guy's still down. If they get up, they come up shootin' at each other."

"You've heard this happen?"

"I've seen it."

"Do the kids make a big deal of it afterward?"

"Well, they just keep it quiet. 'Cause if they talk about it a lot, they know it will get to the principal."

The story related by this boy was not very different from stories told by other children. It revealed the inherently conservative nature of all the local gangs. Each of the groups took their township's boundaries as a marker of their gang's territory. Groups staged "raiding parties" across these boundary lines, but the outline of their home territory was neither challenged nor subject to alteration. The local gangs were classic examples of communal groups whose members were drawn from the local population and whose organization was as viable as it was informal. Such groups also had a reactionary quality.[3] As I indicated earlier, they rose up against real or perceived assaults to the integrity of their group and, by extension, to their community's integrity as well.

The traditional rights and prerogatives of community members had to be defended. Affronts to their pride and sense of proprietorship were "normal" in the sense that they could be expected and were not treated as catastrophes when they occurred. The reactions to such assaults, usually a row of some sort, were equally predictable and restrained. Part barroom brawl and part medieval joust, the rules of engagement were usually well understood and designed to allow the combatants to retain their honor without losing their lives or lands. These were contests, not wars.

No lasting damage was done to either party, but the wholeness of their group and community was reaffirmed through such intermittent tests. It was just as well that the tests were not a daily affair and the demands of fealty were not so onerous as to make being a gang member a full-time job. Children would have found it impossible to satisfy all the demands placed upon them. Furthermore, even though the lines between "regular" life and gang life were blurry, children learned how to balance the competing demands of their roles as family and gang member. Thus, as one boy told me, "when you're with your parents, act regular. When you're outside your home, act like you usually be actin'."

"Like a gang member?"

"Yeahhh."

"How does a gang member act?"

"Tough. Mean. Want to get in stuff out there."

"What kind of stuff?"

"Steal cars. Steal out of stores. Fight a lot."

It was not even required that one be completely faithful to the code that gang members were supposed to follow. There was room, as I noted earlier, for experimenting and downright fakery. One would-be gang member, for instance, spoke with unbridled contempt for another youngster who had claimed to be a Blood. "They took his rag (bandanna), stomped on it and everything, and he didn't do nothin'. He be a real Blood, probably would have shot somebody."

Part of the problem for children and adults under such confusing circumstances comes in trying to identify the "for real" gang members from such fakes. Even when it is pretty obvious that a child is serious about his gang identity there may be a great deal of reluctance on the part of adults to accept the child's declaration. It is not hard to understand why adults would behave in this way. If they were to accept the reality of having a gangbanger in their midst, then they probably would have to do something about it. In that case, their act as a competent adult would have to be at least as convincing as the child's performance as a gang member. Many adults simply are not up to the challenge.

One of the school counselors, a black man, provided me with a good opportunity to see just how hard an adult will work to deny the uncomfortable reality of having gangs around. We were sitting in his office and about to interview a sixth grade boy. The young man looked older and certainly was big enough to be in the junior high school. He could have been held back for any number of reasons. He was, in any case, a good-sized youngster who conveyed a quiet disdain for "the speech" as I introduced myself and told him about the project. The thing that stood out most about the student, however, was that he was dressed entirely in blue. His sneakers, socks, pants, sweat shirt, and professional football jacket were all dark blue. The only other color apparent on him came from the thick gold chain hanging around his neck.

I commented about his outfit. Everything was bright and new.

"Got it for Christmas," he said.

"Lot of blue," I replied.

"I like blue."

"Do you know anything about the Pine Ridge Boyz?"

He should have. We were in the middle of their territory, and they were affiliated loosely with the Crips, whose favorite color is blue.

"No. They around."

"But do you know anything about them?"

"No."

"In fact, we could sit here for a long time and you still wouldn't know anything about gangs. Isn't that right?"

He offered no reply.

"Well thanks for your time. You can go back to your class."

I turned to the counselor after the boy left. He had looked as bored as the student during my brief conversation. I asked him what he thought.

"About what?"

"Do you think the kid's in a gang?" I inquired.

"He said he didn't know anything."

"But what about the way he was 'dressed down' all in blue? Didn't that suggest anything to you?"

"He said he got the stuff for Christmas." The counselor looked mildly perplexed with my insistent tone. "You think he's a gang member?" he wondered aloud.

"Let me put it this way. If he comes to school tomorrow dressed largely in blue and hasn't had the crap beat out of him, then I'd say 'Yes, he's a gang member.' "

"And if he has been beaten up? What then?"

"Then I'd say he'd made a very poor color selection for his ensemble."

This school official may not have been as dim as our conversation suggested. His principal was not particularly supportive of the project. He insisted that gangs were not a problem at his school, and I had little doubt that his attitude had been communicated to the school counselor. The counselor may only have been repeating his boss's views. His refusal to see the obvious made him unsuited for his responsibilities, but why the counselor failed to acknowledge that the young man was a gang member really is not important. The consequences of failing to see the obvious, on the other hand, were important. The young man dismissed so casually by the counselor probably was affiliated with both the Pine Ridge Boyz and the Crips. Had he spoken with us we might have learned a bit more about the way youngsters dealt with such dual loyalties.

I had learned from previous interviews that most youngsters favored their hometown gang. As one boy in a similar position told me, "Really we don't think when we're fighting against Milldale. We don't care if they're Crips or Bloods." The town allegiance tended to be more important.

We also missed a chance to learn how local gangs had come to be "under" the Los Angeles gangs in the children's representation of gang coalitions. I knew from earlier work in the city that the LA gangs had used the network of neighborhood gangs as their wholesale distribution system for selling cocaine. So close had the identification of neighborhood gangs with their Los Angeles suppliers grown that a number of local gangs had incorporated the term "Blood" or "Crip" into the title of their neighborhood group. Thus, the Melrose Boyz might have become the Melrose Crips as its members became more involved in drug dealing.

Gangs in the Fairview School District had not yet changed their names in that way, and perhaps they never would. Yet I had found it interesting that no child had been able to describe the nature of the relation between local and Los Angeles gangs. I had no reason to believe that the Los Angeles gangs were behaving differently in the suburbs; but it was clear that they had not achieved the same success in absorbing local suburban gangs into their large drug franchising operation.

Elementary school children appeared to have little difficulty reconciling their attachment to a neighborhood gang with their expressions of support for non-local gangs. The reason for this probably could be found in their weak personal acquaintances with non-local gang members. Those with personal ties ordinarily had brothers or cousins who were members of the LA gangs. Most children who talked about being a Crip or a Blood were not genuinely serious prospects for membership in those organizations. They were playing at being gang members, and it was simply convenient and dramatic to refer to oneself as a Crip or Blood. Almost every child had heard of them from the media, and these gangs had notorious reputations.

Just how easily young men in the junior and senior high schools would reconcile these attachments remained to be seen. Their ability to do so would have great consequences for their groups and themselves. It would also have broader social significance for the area in which they lived.

The depth of their dilemma is not difficult to apprehend. Gangs are first and foremost communal groups. Most communal groups have a distinctly reactionary quality to them. Their members are tied to the place where they live, and the feeling they have for each other is identified with that place. They are rooted in an almost organic way to this locale, and their sense of loyalty to each other is transferred to the spot of land where they are found and feel comfortable. They are willing to defend that spot, to call it their territory, for this reason. Contemporary youth gangs make a jumble of this logic by laying a pernicious and ruthless commercial enterprise on top of a time-honored way of organizing persons inside a neighborhood or village. It is not that the youth gangs of earlier generations and other ethnic peoples were unfamiliar with delinquent activities. Virtually all of them were. It is rather that the effect of these criminal activities was not as pervasive, violent, or fearfully permanent as that of modern urban and suburban gangs. The effect of these gangs is far more corrosive. They undermine the viability of neighborhoods by introducing a trade that maims and kills indiscriminately. Furthermore, they are tied to a network of groups outside of their area that promises them an unrestricted supply of poison to carry on that trade.

Whether and how well the suburban gangs of the Fairview School District would manage to reconcile the tension between their neighborhood loyalty and business ventures remained to be seen. City gangs might have had little difficulty in becoming retail outlets in a national chain of drug dealing groups, because their neighborhoods were unsettled and their members felt less loyalty to them. This much I had learned from inner-city gang members I had interviewed before moving on to work in the Fairview School District. The suburban gangs probably would have more trouble making this transition or were more reluctant to do so. Their territorial boundaries were fixed by the township lines, taken as legitimate by the youngsters, and treated seriously. Gangs might trade and raid outside of their area, but they had no "credible" claim to the territory through which they moved or tried to conduct business. That was not the case in the city where neighborhood boundary lines and gang territories were less well defined and more vulnerable to claims by "outsiders" intent on expanding their turf and share of the drug dealing market. The size, name, and character of gangs operating under such circumstances might be more easily changed. Trading and raiding also might be more dangerous.

None of this made any difference to the children I interviewed. They were interested only in trying on the role of "gangbanger" and in forming little groups through which their idealized notions of a gang life might become more real. The neighborhood was the first venue for learning these lessons. The local school was not far behind, and in some ways it was more important.

Schools brought most of the community's children together for seven hours each day during the better part of the year. Children were curious about gangs. Some wanted to become members. Others did not. Each school day provided them with an opportunity to explore what it meant to be a gang member along with the school's regular curriculum. Schools also provided students with adults whom they could try to fool about their gang involvement. It was clear that there were times when youngsters were more interested in gangs than they were in their academic pursuits.

"Are you in one of those groups?" I asked one boy.

"Yes."

"Which one?"

"Crip."

"For how long?"

"It ain't like for real."

"Pretending?"

"Yeahhh."

"Why pretend?"

"I don't know. I just like playing."

"Are there other kids pretending, too?"

"Um hm."

"Do you fight Bloods here?"

"Nobody ever told me they was Bloods."

"Then whom are you fighting?"

"Sometimes I fight the ones like if they mess with one of my gang members. Call me 'punk' or 'fag.' Sometimes they call me a cuss word."

"Do you always fight them for doing that?"

"If I'm not in a bad mood, I ain't even goin' to trip offa no name."

"Anyone sell drugs up here?"

He looked surprised. "No. Nobody ever thinks about that up here."

"What if a real Crip or Blood didn't think you were pretending?"

He laughed a bit nervously. "I'm in trouble . . . First thing we're goin' to do is run."

There were a great many children who were pretending to be gang members. They would wear particular types of clothing, talk in exaggerated cadences, and use specific words or hand gestures to give some indication that they were wannabes. They also would linger in specific parts of the school building or on the playground, and they would fight other children who did not belong to their group. Yet they held no serious ambitions about becoming a real gang member and often had given no thought to what they would do if confronted by such a person.

Another boy told me that "every time we have recess, we kinda have . . . not fights, little play fights."

"Crips against Bloods?"

"Yes."

"Do they ever become 'real' fights?"

"If somebody gets scratched . . . or if somebody won't stop hittin', then they get mad."

Yet a third boy noted that there were some serious gang members at his school. He said they were Crips. "I seen 'em jump on Germane."

"Why did they do that?"

" 'Cause Germane was fightin' one of they members."

"How many of these Crips are there?"

"Less than six in the fifth and sixth grades. All come from the same town." He paused for a moment, then he made the following observation. "You got to know who you're fightin'. If you fight the wrong person, you'll get jumped the next day."

A great many children may have been pretending to be gang members, but it was difficult to distinguish them from the "serious" persons and the fake fights from the genuine ones. The descriptions of the children and their activities were quite similar.

There were two ways in which the more serious children set themselves apart. They fought more often and had some experience with criminal activities. Not much of the extra fighting and virtually none of the criminal activity, however, occurred at the elementary schools. Only a few children, for instance, spoke of drug transactions taking place during the school day. One boy reported that a sixth grader had tried to sell him drugs when he was in the school bathroom, but he had reported the event to the principal. The sixth grader was suspended. A second child said that she had witnessed a boy handing money through the playground fence to two older boys and receiving a package in exchange. Little else of that nature was described to me during interviews.

Although the fighting and crime that distinguished the serious wannabe were not in evidence at the elementary schools, those exploits did not go unnoticed. Indeed, it was by telling elaborate stories about fights and criminal ventures that the storytellers enhanced their reputations and other students learned a great deal both true and false about gangs. Children who bragged too often or loudly about these experiences ran the risk of being identified by school staff as someone who should be watched closely and, perhaps, even disciplined. Thus, while students did talk about these activities among themselves, they took some care not to let the resident adults in on the stories. School teachers and staff were more likely to pick out "gang members" from among the students on the basis of the children's tendency to flash hand signals, pass encoded messages, posture shamelessly, and show off money and goods acquired through their criminal ventures. These actions also had the effect for students of reinforcing the stories that they were hearing from each other.

Children in elementary schools paid a great deal of attention to all these signs and stories, rumors and personal observations. They were especially alert to the behavior of sixth graders who were older than other children in their class and of the junior high school students who came to the elementary schools looking for trouble.

A number of children had vivid recollections about "visits" by junior high school students. One boy recalled in an excited tone how groups of the big junior high students came down and "jumped one of our students, one of the kids in my class."

"Why did they do that?" I asked.

"He was this dude's brother, and they tried to jump his brother but they couldn't find 'im. We all knew they was goin' to jump 'im. It happened in the morning before school, in the school yard."

School staff responded as vigorously as they could to incursions by individuals who did not belong at their school. However, there was little they could do when groups of older boys congregated around the school playgrounds after classes had been dismissed. Nor could they do too much about graffiti placed on the the exterior walls of some school buildings. An effort was made to paint over the offending graffiti, but it was hard to keep up with the artists. Surprisingly few graffiti appeared on interior walls of the school buildings.

On the other hand, some school staff also seemed unable or unwilling to see the influence that gang members had on events inside their schools. This was especially apparent in the case of fights between individuals or small groups of boys. The participants usually told teachers that fights had been prompted by students making unflattering remarks about someone's family or friends, and they usually were believed. A number of students made it clear that many fights really were caused by students wearing different gang colors and "standing up for their colors." I was certain that several school counselors had not known this before our interviews.

On a number of occasions school counselors were surprised and upset by what they heard about gangs. One particularly cocky sixth grader had been giving me a hard time. I tolerated his rude behavior for several minutes before turning off my tape recorder. I calmly turned to the woman counselor and asked if I might speak plainly and clearly to the young man. She waved her hand and said, "Be my guest."

I focused my attention on the student and challenged the truth of what he said in a speech that matched and even exceeded the vulgarity of his own. He sat wide-eyed, silent but slack-jawed throughout my presentation. When he finally regained his composure, he turned to the counselor and said, "Can he talk that way to me?"

The counselor just shrugged her shoulders.

"What's it going to be?" I inquired. "Are we going to talk? Or are you going back to your class?"

He stayed and we spoke for a long time. He told us of his previous experiences with gangs in the city. "I never dealt drugs in my life. I ran 'em. Talked to the guys who bought 'em." (He had been a courier between the dealer and customer.)

"How much did you make last year?"

"More than y'all make in a year."

I asked him how much that might be.

"Four thousand dollars."

I asked him on what he had spent all that money.

"Bought clothes, jewelry, other stuff. What the gang needed, I'd help buy some of that."

He then recalled a shooting incident in which he claimed to have taken part. The description of the murder visibly upset the counselor, and I ended the interview shortly after that. We left the school for a few hours and discussed the interview over lunch. "He may have done it," I said. "But remember he was doing an awful lot of bragging."

She was not satisfied. "But still . . ." she said.

"I know. The chances are good that he was there, but I frankly doubt that he did it. He was enjoying the story too much to be the shooter. I know well the city gang he claimed as his own, and they do stuff like that. But you heard the way he talked about one set in his gang leaving the public housing site and beating up any male they could find. Said it was 'crazy.' Said his boys stole cars. That's when he was talking straight. This other stuff about being the shooter is more like 'shooting his mouth off.'"

Our conversation was serious, but I could tell that she was not fully convinced. I did not dismiss her feelings or her judgment. How could I? She had to go back to that school every day. I was just a visitor.

She was as much surprised by the fact that someone so young could have had such experiences as she was by the violence described. Yet these were the very stories that children were sharing among themselves. Part of their "code," indeed part of the code followed by most youngsters as they stumbled and clawed their way into adolescence, was to see how much of their lives they could keep hidden from the adults whose authority they were bound and determined to challenge. Part of what upset the counselors was that we were breaking down a portion of that code and learning important "secrets" that had heretofore escaped their attention.

The young white boy and Junior Disciple named John Baker had provided some insight into this code of silence regarding gangs. I asked him why he did not tell his teachers about the boys in other gangs. His response was that those other boys might then find out about his gang affiliation and tell his teachers or hurt him. He made it clear that it was an unwritten rule among gang members not to "rat" or tell adults about another child's affiliation, even if he were a member of a group strongly opposed to your own.

The code extended to girl gang members as well. One sixth grader told us how older girls had asked her to become a Crip or Disciple and that she had helped them in a number of fights. This came as a surprise to the school counselor.

"Against whom did you fight?"

"Bloods mostly."

"Day or night?"

"Both."

"Are these fights arranged?"

"They're arranged. Some just happen."

"How are they arranged?"

"You send somebody to where they hang out and work it out. They'll spray-paint walls to let people know about it."

"How were you picked out?"

"Some members are friends. Some are relations. They asked me at the beginning of the summer."

"What did they tell you to do?"

"You had to fight a lot."

"Do you consider yourself a gang member?"

"Sometimes."

"Do the kids sell drugs?"

"Yes. Rocks. We get it from the leader."

"How much can you make?"

"Hundreds. The sales take place at night."

"Are drugs sold here?"

The counselor had been sitting quietly, her eyes fixed on the student. Her expression was solemn. She was not prepared for the long silence that followed my question.

"I don't know," the girl finally said in a small voice.

"Any other schools?"

"Morrow Elementary."

"How about here?"

The girl bowed her head and whispered, "I don't know."

"Yes you do," I said softly.

The girl nodded.

"During school or after school?"

"After."

"What are they selling?"

"Rocks."

I excused her at this point, and she quietly left the counselor's office. I looked at the counselor. She had tears in her eyes.

Most children were not so involved with gangs. It was apparent, however, that a number of children had become at least marginally involved. Many more had played at being gang members. They all uttered words used by gang members, flashed hand signals they had learned only recently, and tried to mimic the behavior of gangbangers as best they could. Gangs were a real presence in the schools, if only in the imaginations and play of the children attending classes there. Yet it also was in the elementary schools that a folklore about local gangs was being created and shared among all the children in attendance.

School counselors and principals who had worked in the district for a long time recalled that white youngsters from different towns had always competed against each other and sometimes fought. They had exhibited pride in their towns and defended the community's "honor" as best they could. If one wanted to call the groups of young men who did this "gangs," then gangs had been part of the Fairview School District long before black people had moved into these towns.

This might help to account for why gangs as such were not viewed as exceptional or alarming by many persons, including many of the children with whom I spoke. It almost certainly helps to explain how the boundary line between the world of gangs and the world not of gangs was blurred for the children. Yet the world of gangs described by these children was different from the one recalled by long-time school personnel. The gangs of their present students had a pervasive grip on more aspects of the children's daily lives. The gangs were more violent and were engaged in crimes that brought large sums of money to children far too young to use them responsibly. It was a more dangerous world into which children were being thrust without sufficient guidance or supervision. The children knew that they were being put into such a world, even if the adults did not.

Notes

1 J. M. Barrie, *Peter Pan* (New York: Charles Scribner's Sons, 1980), p. 53.
2 William Golding, *Lord of the Flies*. New York: Aeonian Press, 1975), p. 179.
3 Charles Tilly, "Collective Violence in European Perspective," in H. D. Graham and T. R. Gurr (eds) *Violence in America: Historical and Comparative Perspectives* (Beverly Hills, Calif.: Sage Publications, 1979): pp. 83–118.

3

Coming of Age

Coming of age in our culture is hard work. Boys and girls in their early teens face bewildering changes in themselves and begin to figure out how young adults fit into the world. Some youths fare better than others in part because their talents and circumstances differ. Even under the best of circumstances, however, it can be a time of confusion, experimentation, raging hormones, and bad tempers. Adolescence may not be ideal preparation for adulthood, but it is the last preparation that teenagers get.

The preparation that many youngsters from the Fairview School District got was far from ideal. Their families were kept from some of the better experiences available in this culture, and the youngsters knew firsthand some of its more raw and unsentimental features. A number of the young teens with whom I spoke showed little inclination to be respectful and probably had little familiarity with being treated respectfully by an adult. On the other hand, they evidenced a growing awareness of how to intimidate a stranger and to use insults as armor and violence as a medium of exchange. If one of the keys to a successful adolescence is the opportunity to risk and fail without fearing for one's safety or life, then many of these young teens were stripped of the chance to become a successful adult. They would remain childish, even as they grew older.

The idea that childhood had somehow failed them was not often expressed in conversations that I had with boys and girls in their early teens, but it hung in their words and on many of their faces like yesterday's bad news. It was part of them, and they were not at all certain what they could do about it. They did not lose their innocence so much as had it stolen from them. It happened early, and their loss had a sharp and mean edge to it.

"I think there's a contract out on me," one fifteen-year-old told me.
"Why do you think that?" I asked.
"Some of my boys from the city robbed this dealer, and he knows me."
"So what?"
"So he's put it on me, 'cause if they don't get the person that robbed them, they gonna get somebody that's close to the robber."
"How are you watching out for yourself?" I inquired.
"I don't. When God ready for you to go, you go."

His fear was not misplaced, and his fatalistic attitude was hardly unique among the teens with whom I spoke. Young men in towns more prone to violence have been known to arrange for their own funeral with money acquired from drug sales. Life as they knew it could be nasty, brutish, and short. They merely were arranging for a preordained and prepaid end. The young man I interviewed probably would not be murdered, but hearing that would have made little difference to him or other teenagers like him. They were waiting for something terribly destructive to overtake them, and they were not surprised when bad things happened.

Many of these young men and women had no good place to run and hide, no quiet corner from which to study safely the frenetic comings and goings of their peers. Quiet moments might be stolen in hushed conversations with one's closest friends or in some private spot, but it was hard for many teenagers to catch their breath. They were, quite simply, hung out to cure well before their time.

Their world had few well-defined boundaries. Many more young persons now roamed far from their neighborhoods at all hours of the day and night. They did so with virtually no adult supervision or knowledge. The world was much bigger now, and it also was becoming more complex. There were more and varied contacts with a host of youths known only by the town where they lived or the gang to which they belonged.

If these contacts made the world of young teenagers more complex, they also made that world clearer by providing them with more and better information about those towns and gangs. Although teenagers corroborated much of the information I had been provided by children, their views on many matters were quite different. Five gangs identified by children, for instance, were unknown to junior high school students or were placed in towns outside of their school district. The larger municipal gangs and groups aligned with them were not tied to the Bloods or Crips as children had thought. Moreover, there were three gangs composed exclusively of young women that had escaped the attention of elementary school children. Teenagers had a fuller and more detailed picture of gangs in the area.

There were other ways in which the world of teenagers in the junior high school had become more complex and better clarified at the same time. Young men and women had access to as many drugs and as much money as they wanted. Sex and violence were readily available as well. They also were pretty anxious about the world, but they hid these feelings behind a mask of boastful defiance for their peers and thinly veiled contempt for many adults. All of this made life confusing or at least it presented teenagers with many difficult choices and easy diversions. The clarity came from knowing, in a way that younger children might only have guessed, that gangs were, as one teenage girl put it, "only about drugs, money, and fightin'."

The few discernible boundaries and scattered benchmarks that might limit the extravagant behavior of teenagers or provide them with guidance all tended to reinforce the hard work and mischief of gangs. Adult family members were portrayed as being almost immune to the gang involvement of their teenage children or, in some cases, as seeking to profit from it. Neighborhoods remained the focal point of most gang loyalties and the incubators for illegal economic ventures. The district's only junior high school emerged as a great marketplace for ambitious entrepreneurs and a theater for thugs. It became a sanctuary for gangs, a place tolerant of illegal behavior that undermined the willingness and ability of students to learn and, to a lesser extent, of adults to teach. Such was the world of gangs for young adolescents.

"Drugs, Money, and Fightin'"

"I don't even understand why anybody uses drugs or sells drugs," one boy told me. "They ain't doin' nothing but messin' up other people, and that will just get you in jail a couple of years down the line. Because once you sell for one of them people, they goin' to expect you to sell all of the time."

He had it half right. Virtually everyone who discussed the effect of drugs such as cocaine conceded that it messed people up, but this was of no interest to them. There was real fear and some expectation, on the other hand, that one could go to jail for selling drugs. That stopped more than a few young men from selling altogether and helped to curtail the selling by teens who continued to push drugs. It was not the case, however, that one was expected or encouraged to sell drugs "all of the time." Most teens who sold drugs did so only on a part-time basis. They moved in and out of the drug trade with some regularity and ease. They sold drugs in order to get money. Most stopped selling when there was nothing in particular they wanted to buy or for which money needed to be saved. As with everything, of course, there were exceptions.

I asked one young man how often some of the bigger dealers in his gang sold drugs. "All the time," he replied. "Most of them stopped going to school, too. One of 'em makes a grand a week. I know one who made four grand in one day."

"What about those guys who don't sell regularly? Do they sell for the big dealers in the gang?"

"Yup."

"Do they get in and out of it often?"

"I don't know no one who hoppin' in and out. 'Cuz you know, I know a lotta people who used to do that. But, you know, they got addicted to the fast money there is, you know, when they was stayin' in it." He paused and thought for a moment. "Yeah. Some go in and out."

"Have there been any who got out altogether?"

"Yeah. One guy did it to buy a car. Another guy got out because the police were always watching his house."

"The guys who are sticking with it, why don't they get out?"

"That's all they have to do. They dropped out of school, you know. Most of 'em I know can't even read. I had this other friend. He was jumpin' in and out, too. He almost got killed." Someone gave him peppermint to sell as crack cocaine, and he did not know it. "He sold the peppermint, then got the money. Then the dude came back lookin' for him. Shot 'im, too."

"How much money was involved?"

"Fifty-five dollars."

Another teenager from a different gang told me that in his town gang the "guys who sell regularly, six or so, are Crips. The rest are just Banister Posse."

"The guys who don't do it all the time buy from you?"

"Yeah. We make money selling directly and to our guys; but we make more selling it directly. Our boys keep all of their profits. There' s no second payoff to us [after they buy the drugs]. Everybody takes care of their own money. There's no pooling. The money you put away is for yourself."

"What if one of you is tossed in jail and doesn't have any money to get out?"

"We'll loan it to him."

"He pays it back?"

"If he wants his life."

"How many guys have you sprung that way?"

"None really."

"What drove you guys to sell more often?"

"We just saw how it was. Guys drivin' around in fancy cars and stuff. That's when we got started. My cousin, he knows a Colombian, and he bought some stuff for us. That's how he makes his profit."

"You going to stick with it a long time?"

"No. I can't. The police already know my face."

"How much do you have stashed?"

"About eight thousand. You see I figured on quittin' when I had about fifty thousand."

"What are you going to do after that?"

"I don't know. Probably buy me another car."

"It's a pretty risky business, isn't it?"

"Oh yeah."

A third teenager from yet another gang was more deeply involved in drug dealing and gave no indication of leaving the trade. "It's an everyday thing now," he said. "[In one week] I made twenty-five hundred. At the first of the month you can make like ten thousand, because everybody gets their [welfare] checks then. They come to you and spend their whole check on it."

"What in the hell does a kid your age do with all that money?"

"I bought a car with mine. We stash money, too, for a rainy day. Hundreds of dollars."

"What kind of rain?"

"Like if I'm caught and sent to jail, I might have bond money. I call one of my boys and he comes and gets it. [Otherwise] I keep it just to buy clothes and stuff."

There were many young men who expressed similar ideas and showed no inclination to give up what was for them a fairly lucrative and exciting trade. Some teenagers, however, already were growing weary of drug dealing. As one youth told me, "All of us in the Riveredge sell. I did. I'm trying to quit."

"Why?"

"I want to get my life straight. I started dealing when I was thirteen. I'm fifteen now. I sold every day. We would split it, you know. We bought some marijuana and make bags to sell. Buy a pound for five to seven hundred dollars. Sell it for someone else . . . then sold it for ourselves after paying him off. Made close to thirteen to fifteen hundred dollars profit. My brother split it up for us. We made equal shares."

"What did you do with all the money?"

"Bought clothes. Bought more drugs. Spent it all." He added, "I'm just a little dealer. My brother sells a lot. He gives me money."

Notwithstanding his claim about wanting to straighten out his life, this young man was still in the trade. He was drawn to it through family connections and stayed with it because the ability to spend money became a justification for how he and his brother got it.

If the reports I received were accurate, then most young teens involved with gangs sold drugs at least once in a while. They were not the only youths who sold drugs. Young black men who were not affiliated with a gang sold drugs, and so, too, did a number of white youths. In the case of white teenagers, however, the drugs being sold usually were different types of pills. Cocaine and marijuana seemed to be sold by minority youths, most of whom were tied in with a gang.

Most drugs were sold out on the street. Some youths sold their "product" before the school day began; but the majority practiced their trade in the afternoon once school let out, in the evening, or on weekends. No gang members sold drugs to children, unless the boy or girl intended to sell them. Teens did sell drugs to other adolescents. They sold marijuana cigarettes to individual smokers or sold it in larger quantities to other dope dealers who repackaged it and sold to their customers. Cocaine was rarely sold in bulk. By the time that junior high school dealers acquired it, the cocaine had been processed into "crack" or "rocks."

"I get a rock," one teen said. "Say somebody give me three twenties. They want thirty dollars back. I go out and sell them, those three twenties, give him back his thirty dollars and I can have the rest."

Another youthful retailer indicated that he only sold when we needed the money.

"Why don't you do it all the time?" I asked.

"Why do it, if it ain't necessary and I don't need it?" he replied. "I'm fourteen. I can do lawns for a couple bucks an hour."

"How much can you make selling drugs?"

He replied, "I sell twenties or quarters. Like a twenty is a stone, a rock that costs twenty dollars. A quarter is a rock that costs twenty-five dollars."

"How much of that will be your profit?"

"Five of the twenty. The other fifteen goes to the person who sold you the drugs. He's a Ridge Boy from the high school. He gets his stuff from Bloods."

Every once in a while, of course, a teenage retailer lucked out and sold a lot of drugs. This sometimes happened when white customers were involved. I asked one youth if he had ever sold drugs to white persons. He indicated that he had been warned not to and had almost been caught doing it by the police, but he noted that whites were prized customers.

"There was one time," he said, "a woman pulled up in a BMW, a sharp car. She asked me to go behind the service station with her. She called her husband on the car phone . . . said they wanted three-sixteenths [of an ounce]. All I had was a big old bag of rocks. She gave me five hundred dollars for the whole bag. Then she dropped me off where I had been at and just drove off."

"That was a big day for you?"

"Yeah. I was smilin', but I had to give it back to the guy who I was slingin' for."

"How much did you get?"

"Two hundred. I had a job at the time. I was workin' at [the fast food restaurant], so I took the two hundred and put it in the bank. Save some. Spend some."

"For what are you saving?"

"Gold caps for my teeth."

The money made by this youth and other drug dealers was comparable to that which could be earned in restaurants or, less regularly, by doing neighborhood chores like shoveling snow from people's sidewalks after a storm. Some young men did legitimate work because they liked to earn money. Others held such jobs in order to mask their drug dealing income or to justify their spending habits to adults. One teen told me how two of his friends carried around check stubs from their employer. They showed these stubs to police whenever they were stopped with a great deal of cash in their pockets. This was taken as proof that the money had been earned legitimately. Adults managed to avoid the responsibility of seeing plainly what children were doing by accepting these small pretenses.

Not all of the money "earned" by junior high school students was acquired by "pushing rocks on the block." Some of it was acquired by pushing rocks on the school corridors and in school rest rooms.

"Off the thousand in cocaine that I buy, I'll make three," one young man told me.

"You make two thousand in profits from your investment?"

"Yeah. In school I'll unload about half. I make about two thousand off the stuff I bought. It will last about one week, but I don't do it every week. A couple of janitors and one teacher buy it from us."

He was not the only student who sold drugs in the school, but I found only one other student who claimed to have sold drugs to school staff. I asked a pair of students from the same gang if any staff members bought their stuff. One shook his head. The other nodded and said, "Yeah, the teacher down the hallway."

The first youth looked surprised. "I don't know nothin' 'bout this," he said.

"I do," replied the other student rather emphatically.

It was entirely plausible that two young men from the same gang were not aware, much less fully informed, of each other's business dealings. Each was an independent sales representative for a small but aggressive wholesale distributor whose product happened to be an illegal narcotic substance. Each distributor was free to set his own price for the product he sold or the commission he paid to his sales staff. There was some variation in these amounts, but great swings in the cost to dealers or in their profit margins were not common. There was just too much product available, sales territories were difficult to capture and hold, and the number of competitors was too large. All of these factors kept costs and profits down. A great deal of money was exchanged and circulated at one or another level of the drug trade, but the amounts generated by the street-level dealer were comparatively modest.[1] This, along with the trade's illegal character, helps to account for the comparative secrecy of drug dealers and their ignorance of each other's business dealings.

I asked one young man how long it had been since he had sold drugs.
"Last week," he answered.

"How much money did you make?"

"Fifteen dollars."

"What did you do with the money?"

"I'm gonna buy some gold."

"Chains from a jewelry store?"

"No. Gold teeth. I'm gonna have it done next week."

"How much does that cost?" I asked.

"About one hundred twenty-five dollars. I'm gonna get the money this
week. I might steal a car and retag it."

"You've done this before?"

"Yeah. Every Friday."

"Where do you take them?"

"To my friend's father. He buys them. In one night, we can make three
grand."

"What if you want to keep the car?"

"Then it costs about five hundred dollars to get it retagged."

"Where are you going to get five hundred dollars?"

"Dope. And stealing cars and taking the parts and sell the parts."

"How does that work?" I asked.

"This is how we do it. We steal three cars, and, uh, take one and take
the stuff off it for about a grand. Then we take one and turn it in for the
five hundred dollars. Then we take one and get it retagged. So we walk
away with a car and [the money]. We don't really keep the car. We just
use it to cruise around in and look for another car to steal. We [made] about
one thousand five hundred for two weeks. There are six of us to split the
fifteen hundred."

"Where do you hide the new car?"

"Don't have to hide it, because it's retagged. It's your car now. What
I'm talkin' about doin' is makin' money. That's the point I'm makin'." He
paused for a moment. Then he looked at me with an unfriendly half-smile
and asked, "What kinda car you drive?"

I leaned forward and said, "Makes no difference."

"Whaddya mean?" he asked in a puzzled tone.

I smiled my own half-smile and said, "You'd only touch it once."

The smile left him as he studied my face and tried to figure out exactly
what I meant. He would not bother my car, particularly when there were
so many automobiles out there to steal and houses to break into and rob.
I was no real threat to his various schemes to make money.

He and many other young men acquired hundreds of dollars over a matter
of weeks and up to several thousand dollars over the course of a year. Some
was earned legitimately. Much of it was not. In only a few cases, however,

did young teens manage to acquire and save or "stash" more than a few thousand dollars. None of their business ventures was wildly profitable. If they worked alone, they did not make much money. If they worked as part of a group, the money they acquired was divided among enough persons so that none of them received a great deal. Much money was circulated among a large number of youths, but only a few young men who were major wholesalers like Tyrone Jones made any "real" money from drug dealing.

The manner in which young men handled this money all but ensured that they would eventually have to leave criminal activities for more steady employment or become bigger crooks. These teenagers were profligate spenders. They were so loose with their money that after a while I stopped asking them about their spending habits. Their answers never changed.

"Let's put it like this," one young man said. "Last year I was buyin' a lot of clothes with my three grand. Bought clothes, shoes, everything I thought of. An' another thing they like to do . . . is buying gold teeths. Yeah. People with lots of gold in they mouths."

A second youth said that he spent his money on "clothes, buy some more drugs. Gold, every mother fuckin' thing, that's what."

"Buy yourself a car?"

"Naw. Won't buy cars. Don't got the assets."

"Weapons?"

"Yeahhh . . . got a .25 automatic from a pawnshop. I got my cousin to buy it for me."

He might never use the weapon, but at least he owned a fancy piece of hardware that could be shown off to friends and foes alike. This young man and many others like him made it clear that they really were after "spending money." They bought objects or paid for services that they did not need but wanted and could not otherwise have afforded.

There was much more at stake in their scheming and dealing, however, than the acquisition of "spending money." The conspicuous flashing of money, goods, guns, and drugs was the central feature of a ceremony conducted every day and monitored closely by virtually all youngsters. The object of this ceremony was to enhance the teen's stature in the eyes of his peers. He constructed an identity for himself through the possessions acquired. It was also the easiest way for teens to display publicly the success of their gang and compare it to the success of their rivals.

Such public displays and comparisons took on broader communal significance because all gangs save one were closely identified with a particular town. Even members of the Bloods and Crips subordinated their status as affiliates of these Los Angeles gangs to their more important identity as members of one or another local municipal gang. The importance of such displays as communal exercises was reinforced by the value of the objects being paraded. Many of them were expensive, but they were not at all necessary to the physical comfort of the persons wearing them. Chains, gold teeth, baseball caps, a particular brand of sneakers, shiny jackets, and bandannas were less important as means to cover exposed parts of the body than as signs of a teen's group affiliation and communal loyalty. They adorned themselves in much the same way, or at least for many of the same reasons, as adults do. That such items had greater social significance than they did personal utility was particularly relevant in this case, however, because the owner put himself at some risk when wearing them. Individuals frequently were assaulted or robbed for wearing the wrong color at the wrong place or they increased the chances that law enforcement officers would stop and harass them because they looked like gang members and drug dealers.

At one time or another, a number of youths were involved in illegal activities that brought them money. The number probably was large, but the specific individuals engaged in such ventures apparently changed with some regularity. Those who were involved at any given moment had varying degrees of commitment to these enterprises. Some teens engaged in criminal activities on a routine basis. Others were more marginal participants and restricted their involvement to a few days each month or to the weekends. Teens committed some of their crimes while working alone and some as part of a small group.

All of these facts might be taken as evidence against the idea that much crime was gang inspired. It may not be any more accurate or fair to say that "gangs sell drugs" than it would be to link all teenagers to gangs. Many acts committed by gang members are not necessarily condoned by their group and these same acts are committed by youths who are not gang members. There certainly is good reason to be cautious when painting the gang label on a collection of young adults and some of their behavior.

Much of the information provided by the youths themselves, however, suggests that the gangs as organizations did aid, abet, and reward the criminal activities of their members. Gang leaders provided drugs to novice dealers. Gang members trained would-be dealers and showed them how to hide or spend their earnings. There was marked collaboration among the members of each gang, if not outright cooperation, and they actively resisted the encroachment of "outsiders" into their sales territory. The evidence of group involvement was even more obvious in car robberies and stripping. It was imperative when dealing with automobiles that a number of youths be in the same spot and carry out complementary activities at the same time in order to strip or steal one or more cars. That degree of collaboration among youths may not have been as evident in drug dealing, but it was there nonetheless.

Individuals may have carried out these crimes, but the gang made crime more accessible and efficient for those youths who became involved. The gang also made illegal activities less notorious by weaving them through the community's ongoing routines. Family members and friends, young men and women told me, often were familiar with what neighborhood youths were doing and frequently conspired, if only through their silence, to allow criminal activities to continue. It was through such associations and aid that the actions of local teens were interpreted and came to be tolerated.

The casual adult observer might be excused for ignoring or failing to perceive much of what young men and women did as being "gang related" or being heavily shaped by any kind of "group influence." Adults are not often invited along on car robberies, drug sales, and raiding parties. The participants themselves are not likely to speak with adults about these exploits.

Whatever confusion or ignorance we adults might have about the nature of such activities as being gang related is, in fact, carefully nurtured by the youths themselves. Unless they are asked to elaborate on the way criminal activities are organized, for instance, they leave the impression that only a few friends are involved in such ventures. The number of youths involved, the degree of collaboration among them, and the connection of these persons to a specific group that is rooted in a particular place are all issues that the teens do not raise and most adults do not pursue.

It is not hard to understand why neither the youths nor their adult guardians and overseers go to any great effort to consider such matters, much less to discuss them in detail. These groups of young men and women are not an extraordinary feature on the neighborhood landscape. They are simply "local kids who hang out together." Both the youths themselves and many adults with whom I have spoken hold this view, and there is much that is accurate in it. Yet, as many teens willingly concede, that is not the whole picture. Much more is going on, and part of what is going on could easily put them in physical jeopardy or in jail. So, they are not especially keen on talking about many features of what they and their friends do while "hanging out together."

Young men and women have good reason to foster the impression that they are just "acting like kids." It reassures adults that their children are still engaged in "child-like" activities and do not require more active supervision. It also provides the youths and the adults in most routine contact with them a readily available and believable explanation for whatever transgressions the teens might be caught committing.

Adults often find it difficult to communicate with boys and girls in their early teens. This is particularly true when the subject under discussion touches on their respective privileges and responsibilities. That is why much of the hard work of reaching new understandings or setting new limits is done with little deliberation. A rule is ignored, and no action is taken against the rule breaker. Different clothing is requested or simply shows up one day, and amazingly little grumbling is heard from the parent. The young teen bumps, trips, climbs, and stumbles into uncharted behavioral terrain, and no one seems to take much notice or complain all that long or loudly. Many adults achieve peace and quiet with teenagers in this way. They enter tacit agreements without admitting to themselves or making it clear to the youngster involved. Important decisions are made without a public declaration that big walls have crumbled or civilization as we knew it now laid in ruins at our feet.

The ability of young teenagers to supply accounts and explanations for their behavior that conjure up images of child-like insouciance or ineptitude is vital to this process. It is equally important for the preservation of the illusion that adults accept these explanations and images. If they do not, then the striking of old understandings and the emergence of new ones will have to be done more openly and be taken more seriously. Neither the teens nor the adults behave as if they really want that to happen.

The manner in which teens and adults handled the problem of fighting offers a good illustration of this point. Teenagers fought a lot, and sometimes individuals were hurt pretty severely out on the street. One might have expected adults to worry about this more than they did, particularly in the junior high school where a great deal of fighting took place. Most of the time, however, adults seemed to accept the youngsters' explanation for fights. The teens usually maintained that a fight was over "he-say she-say stuff." Many fights between individuals were precipitated by such comments, and this explanation seemed to satisfy school staff. The teens had learned to use this explanation while in elementary school, and it had worked well. They were not surprised to see that it still worked at the junior high school.

Anyone could have been victimized by the kind of verbal assault that teens called "he-say she-say stuff," and everyone expected such words to provoke a strong physical reaction. Both students and teachers accepted this state of affairs, even though many found it aggravating and stupid. It was just kids acting dumb. School staff apparently did not notice or attributed no significance to the fact that many of these exchanges, perhaps most of them, occurred between teens from different towns. They had virtually no clue that the fights might have had anything to do with ongoing disputes between different gangs.

There were occasions when fights at school involved a number of students. Groups of five or six students might skirmish up and down a corridor for several minutes or simply "jump" an unsuspecting teen as he turned a corner. These events, as one student described them, could be more raucous and less dangerous than street confrontations.

"I was walking down the hall," he said, "and there were a whole lot of dudes . . . and they hit us, you know. And we fought back. A whole lot of us came. It was just knockin' everybody out. I got thrown down the steps. Then I got back up and started fightin'. One of the teachers came in and everybody broke."

"After all of that," I asked, "you still don't consider yourself a member of the group that got jumped?"

He shook his head. "No. But it's like if two dudes jump this one person I know, I'm gonna jump in and help him."

It was not a coincidence that the persons who had been jumped came from his hometown and were members of the local gang. The young man telling the story simply had behaved in a "patriotic" way when he rose to defend his fellow townsmen. School staff accepted the mildest interpretation of these events, dismissing them as nothing more than "fights between kids from different towns." It never occurred to them to ask the students who were routinely suspended after such brawls whether anything more significant was going on. It never occurred to the students to disabuse the adults of their comfortable prejudice. The fights were prompted by ongoing disputes between gangs from different communities. What started on the streets carried over into the school.

Two types of disputes led to fights between groups of young men or women. There were disagreements revolving around the activities of gangs. These might entail nothing more significant than the color of clothing worn by different teens. Or, these might involve something more serious like the incursion of one gang into the drug dealing territory of a second gang. A second kind of dispute was of a more general sort and involved long-standing rivalries between different towns.

The problem was that it could be difficult to determine where a disagreement between two gangs ended and bad feelings between the youth of two towns began. Gang members often initiated these fights and always took an active part in them. "Gang fights" tended to be smaller and meaner affairs. Weapons often were carried, flourished, and used during such confrontations. "Community fights" tended to be larger and noisier events, but they were far less likely to involve the use of guns or weapons or to end with serious injuries to anyone.

Two young men described different gang fights they had participated in or witnessed.

"I saw the leader of the Pine Ridge Organization get shot in a big fight," one teen said. "He got shot in the arm. It went through, came out."

"Why did the fight occur?" I asked.

"The Vista Village say the Pine Ridge stole from them. Yeah, now they gettin' scared of Pine Ridge."

"Why are they scared?"

"See, the Pine Ridge got respect. Still, people might don't think it. But when it all boils down, Pine Ridge got respect. Only time we get ruthless is when somebody tries to attack us. That's when we come sliding down shootin' up houses and stuff."

"Is that what happened with Vista Village?"

"Yes."

Another youth stated that gang fights were so frightening and violent that "half the time they don't know they been shot. They get into the car and see all the blood."

It was just like the previous week, he added. "We were down at [a public housing complex in the city], and we shot up a couple of those boys down there. They come out here and tried to take over our dope scene. There were about four cars of us and we had 38 s . . . High Top, he had an Uzi. They fired into the buildings. It was early Sunday morning. One of their boys come out here and tried to sell some rock. So next time they'll know not to come into our territory. They might come out again. That's why we're waitin' on 'em now."

Fights between groups of young men from different communities, like the one at the junior high school that I described earlier, involve more persons and require no real provocation. The typical fight probably has a great deal in common with raids by one gang into an opponent's territory. The element of surprise seems crucial in these engagements. As one youth described it, "there was about ten of us walking home and it was just unexpected that all of them came out there by the little bus stop."

"How many were there?"

"There was about fifty Rose Terrace kids over there, junior high and senior high, and we didn't see one of them. They just came out on us, not realizing that there were would be [so many more] of them on each of us. But it really wouldn't matter because we knew that we was doin' somethin' good. We was goin' to fight back instead of runnin' . . . and show them that we was no punks."

"They beat you pretty badly, huh?"

"Let's say they won. Really they didn't win because there was less of us."

Both groups apparently had made their point, and doubtlessly they would fight again. Insofar as one could ascribe a purpose to these ongoing skirmishes, I think the following exchange sums it up nicely.

One young woman told me that gangs fought "to see what gang's the toughest. To see what hood's the toughest." I asked her whether she ever had been in one of those fights and she answered, "Yes." Then I asked her whether anything ever was resolved as a result of one of those fights. She shook her head and said, "No." I believe that she had it right.

"Don't Know What They Wannabe"

Young men and women with whom I spoke about gangs were preoccupied with stories about fighting, drug dealing, and all the money that teens acquired and spent by virtue of their involvement in illegal activities. It also was clear that a good number of youths from each town were involved with their local gang. Some were trying on the identity of a gang member and operating at the margins of the local gang. Others were more fully committed to their gang and had established a solid identity as a gang member. Even among a portion of the young men who acknowledged being gang members, however, there was uncertainty about whether their decision to be an active member was a good one or how long they would remain actively involved.

It was hard to determine with any precision how many young men and women should have been called marginal or active gang members. The numbers surely were greater in the bigger towns than in the smaller towns. My conservative estimate, based on what the students at the junior high school told me, would put fewer than two dozen young men in the smaller town gangs and fewer than seventy-five young men in the larger town gangs. These numbers would have included both junior and senior high school students and were corroborated by senior high school students when I spoke with them.

Insofar as these estimates were conservative and represented an under counting of the young men involved with gangs, then at least 350 males were involved with gangs. This would have represented just over one-third of the 1,056 males attending the junior and senior high schools. It would not have included active gang members who had dropped out of school.

There were about a hundred more females than males in the junior and senior high schools. The number of young women involved with gangs, however, would have been much smaller than the number of male gang members. There were only five known female gangs, and girls were not reported to be active in them after they entered high school. Each female gang probably had no more than a dozen members, but those estimates were based on pretty sketchy reports.

Excluded from these counts are the young men and women in each town who would have assisted their fellow townsmen in a fight against a different community. I have no reliable estimate of how large these numbers may have been. I was given estimates for the larger towns that ran as high as "a hundred or more," but I suspected that these were highly inflated counts. Gang members were the most active fighters, in or out of school. Other young persons were sometimes drawn into fights and were quite willing to jump into fights when their fellow townsmen were outnumbered by their opponents.

There were occasions when it was hard to tell the difference between gangs and young men who simply tried to help their friends. One teen attempted to assure me that the youths at whose side he sometimes fought were not gang members, even though I had been informed that some in his group sold drugs in an organized way.

"Our parents," he said, "know it's not really a gang or nothin' like that. They know . . . we just help each other fight. [People] just call us one gang, an' they would call another city a gang. Something like that. But they really don't know what the differences are."

"What are the differences?"

"Difference is you got people that will really help each other . . ."

"But what is a gang?"

"What I consider a gang is you been initiated an', ah, you wear a certain color or somethin' . . ."

"And you guys?"

" 'Cuz it's like if they fightin' us, they fightin' one of us and they's about three of them. They will know they have somethin' on they hands, if they started it and we didn't. The one of us will come back and tell the rest of us . . . An' long as he fight for himself, he know he got backup. We will go help him. They, it's like they would try to call our side the weak side 'cuz we don't shoot or nothin' like that. We got close friends over there. So it's like, if we do fight their side, we won't hit our close friends. We just hit the ones we know be causin' somebody trouble. The close friends of ours won't be hit."

This conversation was interesting on several counts. The young man spoke at some length about the communal origins of his group and the fact that the members' parents knew and accepted much of what the boys did together. Whether the parents knew that some of their children also were engaged in criminal activity I did not determine. It is entirely possible, however, that they did not know.

Even more important, to my thinking, were his comments about what did not happen in fights with groups or gangs from other towns in which he and his cohorts had friends. The idea that communal brawls were not so wild and undiscriminating as they might have appeared is interesting. It indicates that young people were capable of exercising far more restraint than many school personnel certainly imagined was possible. It also suggests that friendship and perhaps even familial ties across towns and between different gangs could temper disputes and limit the levels of violence that accompanied such confrontations. I had received testimony to this effect from some elementary school students who talked about shooting pistols more to frighten their adversaries than to injure them. Some students also talked about the way boys allowed themselves to be dissuaded from fighting by their girlfriends. There would be other reports of how seemingly reckless youths sought to limit the violence associated with gangs without violating whatever code of honor compelled them to fight.

It was especially instructive to hear such stories from young teens at the junior high school, because they often did seem out of control. There was more to becoming a gang member or remaining a gang member than most adults knew and most youngsters were able or willing to articulate. Even at this age, many young men and women were trying to figure out how much of themselves they were willing to give to a gang.

An unknown number of young men at the junior high school were still playing with the role of "gang member." It was important that they did this while in school, because there was an audience to observe the displays and the likelihood of being hurt severely at the school was slight. The consequences for doing this on the street would have been far greater. As it was, one young man from the junior high school simply dismissed the teens who behaved this way as "perpetrators."

"Some of 'em don't know what they wannabe," he observed. "One day, like a month ago, that's when Crips really was the biggest. They say they was Crip. Now that more people want to be Bloods, they'll switch and wanta be a Blood. They don't know what they be doin'. I guess they think gangs are cool. They be dressed all in blue an' stuff, and have their pictures taken like they Crip. You know."

"You mean when they pose in a group and are holding weapons?" I inquired.

"That's it," he answered. "That's how it got started."

I asked another teen how many "for-real" Bloods there were at the junior high school. " 'Bout two," he responded. Still, he was not sure how anyone really could know.

"What I don't understand," he said, "is how can you say somebody real when . . . you don't see 'em get initiated. They could be lyin', sayin' they dopin' this and that."

"Well, then, how can you tell?"

"Tattoos on the shoulder."

Yet a third young man stated that "the boys just wannabes. They don't know half the stuff of the boys from California. They come up here sayin' 'What's up Blood?' 'What's up Cuz?' and all that stuff. Half of the boys doin' it because they friends doin' it. When they by themself they a totally different person. I don't think nobody goin' to this school really initiated. They're just perpetrators."

The term "perpetrator" is used routinely to describe young men and boys who pretend to be gang members. It is a term of derision and is intended to convey the impression that the individual assigned the label has violated a rule that is important to his peers. Youngsters do not use the term in precisely the same way as a police detective might, but to the teens a "perpetrator" is guilty of having committed a crime of some sort.

The crime being perpetrated is one of willful misrepresentation, impersonating a gang member. It is taken seriously because the reality of what it means to become a gang member has become more firmly fixed in the minds of young men and women. They realize that being a gang member can mean living fast, living hard, and living short. It is not so much that teens respect gang members as persons, although many youngsters clearly were attracted to the money and "glamour" associated with being a member. It is rather that they are mindful of the danger attached to being a member and take seriously the responsibilities that a young person like themselves assumes upon gaining entry to that world.

I spoke to two young men about being recruited into their gang. It's just "people who you know just down with you. First, you gotta be around them for awhile and then when it come down to that point, like when we come down to that fighting point and they down with you, then we'll see about gettin' into it." The other youth nodded his head in agreement. He added, "Like some people hopefully want to be down with it, but they ain't. 'Cuz at a time when it's time to fight, they be movin' out the way. Understand?"

I nodded my head. Then I asked the last youth who spoke why he did not have a tattoo on his arm like his friend did. "I just sorta chill waitin' for to get mine," he said. "'Cuz I heard it hurts. So I'm just chillin' for awhile ... but I'm gonna get mine." The first youth nodded his head in agreement. He added that his "hurt for 'bout a week."

The scarring was crude and left broad welts on the upper arm. While being marked in this way is associated with a youth's coming of age in different cultures, no one with whom I spoke tied the scarring to any ceremony, and many gangs did not require it at all. For those who carried such markings, however, they stood as a powerful reminder of the kind of pain and sacrifice that members were expected to endure for their gang.

There were other ways to exhibit loyalty to one's gang. "Sometimes," one young man said, "they ask you if you got the wrong colors, if you sweatin' the wrong colors. You sleepin' in the bloody bed? What dog you sweatin'? What up with all that scratch?"

"Bloody bed?" I asked.

"Hangin' with the wrong crowd."

"Dog sweatin'?" I continued.

"You flyin' them colors?"

"Up with all that scratch?"

"What up with your colors? Like if you a Blood and you got on all red, the Crips say 'What up with all that scratch?' Yep. 'What's up with all that flue [blue]?" Bloods be sayin'. 'What up with all that flue?'"

If a person were confronted in this way, while wearing the wrong color, he probably would be beaten severely. It might not even matter that he obviously was not a gang member. As one teen stated, "two months ago they were jumpin' people who had blue on."

"Did it matter if they were white or black?" I asked.

"No, only if they were wearin' blue. They just beat up on 'em. There be a blob of them, and they just pick on one person."

The danger for young men at this age went well beyond a physical beating. They knew that they could be shot or maimed as a result of such an attack out on the street. A few drew parallels with the movie *Colors*, which dealt with California gangs.

"Like in *Colors*, that Crip that got the Uzi . . . said he was going down for his colors and started shootin' . . . he didn't care if he got killed or not."

"Do you care, if you're killed?" I asked.

"Can't do nothin' but die! How you goin' to care? Can't stop it."

"Do you try to avoid it?"

"Yeah. I mean I don't try to kill myself, but it's gonna happen in the long run anyway."

"Does it increase your status, if you shoot someone during a fight?"

"Yeah. I shot at somebody . . . but I missed . . . One time we was all in Roosevelt school yard . . . when Stupid and them had that fight. They pulled out guns an' started shootin', fightin'. Bats. They brung bats, pieces of gates, barbed wire. Had everything. They was fightin'."

Another youth described a drive-by shooting conducted by one gang with which he was familiar. "They stand up for they colors when they drive by. They get out of the car . . . They'll drive by shootin', come back around 'cuz they know [their opponents] will come out of the house, then [they] step out of the car. They down for their colors."

The dangers are real, even for young men like the thirteen-year-old with whom I spoke who, while claiming to have been initiated into the Crips, viewed himself only as a marginal member of the gang. His name was Michael Livingston. I asked him what would happen were his identity as a Crip known to many students. Michael answered, "I'd get beat up." I then asked him how he had come to be a Crip.

"I usually go down into the city with a couple of my friends," he said. "Then one night they said we want to introduce you to a couple of our friends, and I said alright. They said this is the head honcho of the Crips in the [metropolitan] area. I said, 'What's up?' And he say, 'would you like to become a member?' And I said, 'Yeeehh.' Then they initiated me."

"Of what did the initiation consist?"

"Walkin' down the strip of an area and bein' beat up."

"How many kids?"

"Just about the whole gang. Twenty or thirty."

"How badly hurt were you?"

"Uhm, just a couple of bruises and a bloody lip."

"How long ago was that?"

"About a year and a half ago."

"What do you do as a Crip?"

"Go around fightin' Bloods, Vice Lords."

"You've been in some big fights?"

"Yes."

"Any other white kids in these fights, or are you the only one?"

"Probably two or three. One of them's from your university. He's about nineteen or twenty."

"Do you become involved in drug dealing?"

"Nah, I stay away from that. Steal cars and all that stuff out of cars. I'm just with them when they do it."

"Do you get any of the money from the sales?"

"Yes."

"About how much during an average week?"

"About fifty, because I'm on the outer edge. I'm not deeply involved."

"What do you do with the money?"

"Save it up. Spend it on vacations."

"Do you live with your parents?"

"Grandfather."

"Does he know you're into this?"

"No."

"How do you keep it from him?"

"Just never tell him."

"Does he know that you have extra money?"

"No, because I never show him."

"So, you lead a pretty anonymous existence inside your grandfather's house. Come and go as you wish?"

"That's right. I'm in the house about midnight, one o'clock. When he's in bed."

"So, you have no curfew?"

"Not really."

"Any other white kids at this school involved?"

"No. Most of them stay clean away from it. I saw one white kid pay a Blood for some protection."

"How much money?"

"About twenty-five dollars."

"For how long is this good?"

"About a day or two."

"Do many white kids pay protection money?"

"About half of them do."

"It can't be that high," I stated. "These kids don't have that kind of money."

"I don't know where they're gettin' it from, but I see them givin' twenty-five or thirty dollars every two or three days."

"Do the bangers keep coming back for more money?"

"Yes. And some of them are just beatin' up the kids for it and stuff."

"I don't understand."

"They beat them up *and* take their money."

"You don't pay protection money, do you?"

"No."

"Why not?"

" 'Cuz I got all the protection for free I need."

"Which is?"

"Well, at home I got a gun that I carry on my leg." He rolled up his pant leg and showed me where he wrapped the holster around the calf.

"For outside of school?"

"Uh huh."

"Ever have to use it?"

"Not yet. Hopin' I ain't."

"And in school?"

"I just got other members to protect me."

"The other Crips?"

"Yeah. We just sorta pass each other in the hallway and pretend that we don't know each other. I don't hang around with any black people."

"So the whites that pay are some of the littler ones?"

"Uh hum."

"What about the girls? Do they pay?"

"No. They don't mess around with the girls."

"When do you see your black friends? After school?"

"I'll put my stuff down, wait 'til four or five o'clock ..."

"Where do you eat dinner?"

"Most of the time I don't even eat dinner."

"And your grandfather does not ask where you are going?"

"Nope."

"You get in ..."

"At about one-thirty in the morning."

"Your friends drop you off?"

"No. Most of the time I walk in ... from Main Street in the city. It's about five or six miles. I'm pretty used to it."

"Are you afraid?"

"Sometimes, but not all the time."

This young man might not have been frightened all the time, but some young men more deeply involved in their gangs were. One teen described how he and a close friend were trying to "back their way out" of drug dealing.

"I'm goin' to be real with ya," he said nervously. "I'm scared to get caught." He added that both black and white cops from his town would take his drugs and money from time to time without arresting him. It was too much for him to handle.

"How much have you stashed?"

"I don't be countin' it. There's a lot. I just, I just hold it. I don't spend it."

"Somewhere between ten and twenty thousand?"

He nodded his head as if to say "yes."

"What about your friend? Same thing?"

He nodded again.

"What about the kid at the high school who you claim is making fifteen thousand a week? Does he have others selling for him like you?"

"Yeah. I think that other people's sellin' for him."

This teen did not tell me who the big dealer was. There were only a few young men enrolled at the high school, however, who were "dealing weight." When I reviewed my notes at the end of the project, I suspected that he probably had been talking about Tyrone Jones or one of Tyrone's closest associates.

There were at least a few teens from other gangs who also said that they wanted to leave gangbanging and drug dealing. They, too, were anxious about ending their involvement. They had seen enough violence and wanted no more of it.

"I used to be a member of the Bloods," one youth told me, "but I left it about a month ago."

"Why?"

"It hit me that I was only killin' members of my own race." He added that when he said this to other members of his gang, "they didn't think nothin'" about it.

"Do they know yet that you're leaving?"

"No. I really haven't told them. They'll be somethin' I have to do to get out. The procedure is that you have to kill somebody in your family . . . or get beat up by a whole bunch of them. I'm goin' to choose to be beaten up."

Another young man named Jamal asserted that both he and his best friend were going to try to back away from the Crips. "We wanta get out," he said. "We tired of it, all that fightin'. Get our lives straight."

Jamal's friend added, "It's gonna be hard gettin' out."

"How do you do it?" I asked.

"We ain't been hangin' around," he replied. "You know, this ain't worth dying for."

"What made you want to stop?"

Jamal offered an answer. It was "after one of my boys shot this boy from Riveredge in the head, everything just slid back. Everybody just stopped. We just been fightin', then the boy start shootin' . . . Everybody got scared. I'll still gangbang every once in awhile. Show my colors. But I don't like to go up to everybody and say, 'Yo man, what's up?'. I'll still be a Riveredge Boy and Crip. I just won't be known for it."

"Will you still sell drugs regularly?" I inquired.

"No. I don't think so." He thought for a moment and added, "I might 'til I get a job. I'm trying to get me a job now."

Jamal's friend then spoke. "I realize it ain't worth it, being shot up or going to jail or something. You can back out, but you can't get out." Jamal "brought it to me. He said, 'Man, I'm nothin' but fourteen and I can't handle it.' And I say, 'I see what you're sayin' man.'"

"What do you stop doing when you're backing out?"

Jamal answered this time. "I used to go everywhere throwin' up gang signs. I still wear my colors. I just don't wear them every day. I used to wear blue every day. I had blue shoes. I had blue everything."

"Won't other persons in your gang realize what you're doing?"

"It won't matter. I ain't scared. But when I've [been] doin' shooting and stuff, I just be thinkin', 'What if I'd had got shot and died?' It wasn't worth it. I ain't ready to go to jail."

"Does anyone in your family know about this?"

"My mother told me, 'Don't be usin' drugs. They can mess up your life.' I see how the people come to me, askin' me for drugs. Sometime they don't have no money. They ask for some on credit. They rob for you. They do anything."

"If you feel this way," I asked, "why do you sell drugs to them?"

"They messed up they life," Jamal answered without hesitation. "It's they mistake. They did it to themselves."

"You said you have a little brother, right?"

"Yeah."

"Well, what does he think about all of this?"

"He be tryin' to do it, too. And I be tellin' him, 'Don't do that stuff.' He doesn't believe me. He be tryin' to hang out. But every time I see him, I give him five dollars and tell him to go somewhere 'cause I don't want him around me. I don't want him to see what I'm doin'. 'Cause if he do it, I don't think he be as smart as I was. I don't think he'll want to stop, because at first I didn't want to stop because I saw how all the money was comin'. It's too fast, too fast. I'm only fourteen. I ain't ready to go to jail."

"I understand," I said, "but are other kids like your brother going to stay away from it? How many wannabes are at this school?"

"There's a lot of them, 'cause they look at us as role models. A lot of them want to be like us."

"Do you have to recruit them?"

Jamal shook his head. "Most of the time they come to us."

However true this was for teenage boys, it seemed no less true for teenage girls who became gang members. I mentioned earlier that gang-banging for girls reached its height during the early teen years. A good many young women associated with gang members, but their number was substantially less than that for the teenage boys involved with gangs. There were only five independent female gangs, and the number of girls in any of these groups was estimated to be no greater than fifty. Most young women seemed content to be viewed as "girls who hung with the gangs."

Judging by what young men and women told me, it seemed that girls engaged in many of the activities that teenage boys undertook. The difference was that young women did not do as many of these activities as often or as aggressively as did young men. It was for this reason that they appeared to submit to the boys' leadership and mimic the boy's behavior.

I was told that female gangs enjoyed fighting almost as much as male gangs did, and they fought for similar reasons.

"We fight when we have to," one teenage girl told me.

"What's going to prompt a fight?"

"Some of 'em over they boyfriends, or call each other names. Sometimes it's over jackets. Somebody break into somebody locker and take their jacket."

"Outside of school do you hang around with other members of your gang?"

"Sometime. I have friends in other [girl] groups. We don't fight them."

"Will your friends from other groups help you in a fight against another gang?"

"If they have enemies in that group, yes."

"Is there anything else that causes a fight?"

"When they try to run it all."

"What does that mean?"

"They want to rule over you. And, you know, they hit you and they don't want you to hit 'em back. They try to be the biggest."

"Will any of the high school girls from your town come down and help you in a fight?"

"Sometimes. We call 'em a day before it happens." Other groups, she noted, also do this with their senior high friends.

Another young woman said that girls used "their fists, maybe rocks . . . or a knife" in these fights. I found no one who had ever heard of a teenage girl using a gun, however. This did not stop them from being fierce fighters. Several young men commented on the fighting prowess of female gangbangers. One or two boys even said that they would rather fight other young men than some of the girl gang members.

It seemed from what the young women told me that each female gang was aligned closely with the male gang from its town. Although they did not often fight alongside the boys, the girl gang members did choose the same "enemies" as their male counterparts and fought young women from those other towns.

Part of the motivation for "falling together" involved mutual protection. "There was a whole bunch of girls that wanted to fight us," one young woman recalled. In fact, "they wanted to fight me; but since I was cool with some other girls here, we just all got together and fought the girls from the other town. It was just safer to be together. We've been together for three years now."

Young women who formed their own gangs "fell together" for the same reasons teenage males did. As one young man said, "It's like . . . most of them real tight and they stay in the neighborhood and they grow up with 'em. So that's basically how it is." Their neighborhood and schools put them together, and they developed strong bonds of friendship by acting as a group.

Yet fighting was not the only activity engaged in by girl gang members or girls associated with male gangs from their home town or elsewhere. These young women also worked and played with the teenage boys. They worked in the drug trade and socialized with young men from the local gangs. "Socializing" might entail nothing more than going together to parties or the same school function. It also could involve dating and sexual relations. Although there were substantial variations among gangs regarding sexual practices, everyone acknowledged that females involved with gangs in some way were much more sexually active than girls who were not involved with gangs.

One young man said that girls in the gang aligned with his own group were "cool." He added that "usually they either go with a dude that's in the Milldale. Or, sometimes they just be hangin' 'cuz they friends be goin' with a person that's in the Milldale."

"Do you keep more than one girlfriend?"

"Naw. You ask if she have any friends. If she ain't got no friends . . . then you'll still be with her."

"How many of the Milldale Girlz have you had?"

He laughed. "I won't say," he replied.

"A number?"

"Yeah," he said laughing, "a number."

The young man sitting next to him said, "I think I had about two from over there."

"Will the Milldale Girlz do it with guys from other gangs?"

"Naw," said the first youth. "Sometimes they won't even do it with the Milldale . . . it ain't like they just be scared and say 'here'. They'll stand up for theirs."

"Do the girls sell drugs?"

"Some of 'em. It's just the boys got more clientele. Meaning, uh, more people know the boys more than know the girls." Even among gang members, boys still had greater freedom to roam and to meet new persons. Girls were less mobile and did not have the personal contacts needed to carry out a more ambitious drug dealing trade.

A youth from another gang observed that teenage girls were "the holders. They'll hold [drugs] for you. We'll say, 'The police after me. Will you hold this for me, and I'll come back and get it later.' And they'll say, 'Yeah, I'll hold it.' It's like a carrier. Yeah. They like a safety deposit box."

I asked several young women and men how much they were paid for serving as "holders" or "couriers." One teenage girl said that when money was exchanged it was "probably a hundred dollars. Somewhere in a hundred, two hundred dollars for about a week's work." She knew two girls who did this.

On other occasions, more was involved than a simple business transaction. It often was the case that young women who helped teenage boys with drug dealing were the boys' girlfriends. As one young man put it, girls in the school would "keep it in their lockers."

"Why?" I asked.

"Because they're gang members, I guess."

"Do they get money for keeping it for the boys?"

"Not really."

"Is it because they're the boy's girlfriend?"

"Yes."

These young women often received presents from boys, but it was not merely because they sometimes held the boy's drugs. Several gang members described the arrangement in words similar to those used by a young man named Cleonus. I asked him if girl gang members were more popular than other girls. He replied, "In some cases they is. Yes, you could say that."

"Are they more sexually active, too?"

"Oh yeah," Cleonus responded strongly.

"Do guys pay them afterward?"

"I haven't heard of that."

"Give them presents?"

"Presents. That's a dope dealin' thing, presents."

"What about regular boyfriend and girlfriend stuff? They hang around with you. Are they more likely to have sex with your guys?"

"Yes," Cleonus said.

"Will they receive presents for this?"

"Not really. 'Cuz it's like in a sense they belong to us, you know."

"Do they view themselves as belonging to you?"

"Uh huh. In a sense."

Most young women stayed close to home and had sexual relations only with males from their local gang. This custom was not adhered to by all young women, however. While one young man acknowledged that sexual relations between boy and girl gang members occurred "quite a bit," he denied that these contacts occurred exclusively among young persons from the same town.

"No," he objected. "The girls will have sex with boys from different towns. It's not really allowed for people to go with people in they main territory. It's always with the other side that don't like each other. I've never known no one to go with anyone in their territory."

"Is this a problem for the guys in your hood?"

"Not really."

There were occasions when it was a problem. Young women frequently were portrayed as flirtatious troublemakers who provoked fights between boys from different towns. They learned to use their bodies to acquire status among their peers and rewards from young men, but they managed to heighten ill feelings and tensions between groups by behaving in this way. This did not seem to concern them a great deal. They were viewed as being far more interested in the rewards that came from such activity.

One young man captured it nicely when he indicated that these girls had more status than those who were not in gangs or attached to gang members.

"Are they more popular?"

"Yeah."

"Are they more sexually active?"

"Yeah."

"Big time?"

"Yeah."

"You've got a dirty grin on your face. What does that mean?"

"That's all they think about," he replied. "Gettin' laid . . . that's all they think about. And they think about fightin'."

"Is it an advantage for them to have sex?"

"Uh hum."

"Are the girls not in gangs as sexually active?"

"No."

"With whom are the girls having relations? Male gang members?"

"Yes, other boy gang members."

"Besides status what do the girls get out of this? Do they get money?"

"About two out of three times they do . . . as a present afterwards."

"How much are we talking about?"

"Well, if you're lucky, about twenty-five, thirty dollars."

"So the girls trade sexual favors for money?"

"Yup."

"Do their parents know about this?"

"Noooo."

A young woman confirmed that the girls who strutted around school did receive more attention and were sexually active. She also knew four girls at the junior high school who had become pregnant and aborted the fetus.

"How old were they when they started?" I asked.

"Around twelve or thirteen."

"Do their parents know?"

"Some parents don't even care. Some parents don't even take their daughters to the doctor or anything."

Another young woman acknowledged that "a couple of girls had jobs in restaurants and clothing stores, but most did not. She would not tell me what she and her friends gave boys in exchange for the money they received. I then asked her if anyone ever had sexual intercourse at school. She nodded her head and told me how one couple had "made it" on the steps going up to the third floor.

"What did the other kids think?"

"It was trifling. How nasty can you get?" she replied.

"Was it rape?"

"No. Girlfriend and boyfriend at the time."

Other students confirmed the story, but observed that such encounters did not happen often. "Once last year and once this year," one youth told me.

"Was it rape?"

"No. They both wanted to do it," he answered.

"Did kids at the school know about it?"

"Yes."

"What did they think about it?"

"They don't care."

This was not true. A number of students did care how their peers behaved. Young women seemed particularly put off by the conduct of teenagers affiliated with gangs, but they did not complain to school staff. They believed themselves to be in a place where drug dealing, fighting, and occasional sexual encounters were tolerated. Teenage girls who were involved in gangs of their own or with male gang members postured themselves differently. They did not speak of themselves or behave as if they had much credibility and worth independent of that ceded to them by teenage males who were part of a gang. The fact that other youths reportedly acknowledged the status of female gang members or young women attached to male gangs, and the money or "presents" they acquired, merely reinforced that state of dependence.

Families, Neighborhoods, and School

These young teens were learning many important lessons about themselves, and these lessons were shaped and reinforced by what happened in their families, neighborhoods, and school. They did not tell me everything they were learning; but they did share some valuable insights into what it meant to be a gang member in each of those settings. The stories and lessons were remarkably similar.

I draw attention to this consistency because "the gang experience" did not vary greatly for young men or women across the different gangs whose members I had occasion to interview. More important, I believe, was the apparent consistency in the lessons they learned in their families, neighborhoods, and school. There was no great social chasm separating these important institutions and the work they did. Clues to what lay ahead for many young men and women were gleaned from each, and so, too, were notions about appropriate and inappropriate conduct. In most instances, gang members and wannabes heard similar messages from their families, neighbors, and school teachers. The clues they discerned and the notions they picked up in each spot resonated all too clearly and well.

I asked one young man about the living arrangements of teens who sold drugs regularly. "Do they live at home?" I inquired.

"Yeah," he replied. Moreover, most parents knew their child was slangin' drugs. "Most of 'em ... crack addicts. The [dealers] whose mothers ain't crack addicts give their mothers some money."

"Do the mothers ask for money?"

"If they know that they son's sellin' drugs and, you know, [he] made no attempt to give 'em money, they might ask for some money."

"What do the parents do with this money?"

"Buy cars and clothes and food."

"Do their parents try to get their kid out of it?"

"Not now. Not them."

Another teen noted that "sometimes you be stayin' with your family one out of every five to ten months, and they let their kids stay in the house, but they got to pay ... rent. Some have to pay five hundred a week to stay at their parents' house. I can think of about three right off hand who pay ... rent."

"Do parents charge their kids rent, if the kid's not selling drugs?"

"No."

"Parents know their kid's out until the early morning selling this stuff?"

"Yeah."

"Don't they care?"

"All they know is that they're gettin' their money."

"What happens when parents find out and don't like it?"

"Then you gotta move out of the house, move in with one of your friends."

"Do you know anyone who has done that?"

He bowed his head a bit and said, "Yes."

If there was a pattern in which parents cared and which ones did not care, I did not discern it. Two young men from the same gang, for example, had quite different experiences. One had acquired twenty dollars by selling drugs the morning that I spoke with them, and I asked what he would do after school.

"Go home and chill in the crib," he responded. "Make some more money."

The second youth observed that he had stopped selling dope, at least for the time being. "I ain't did it in about three weeks . . . I stopped . . . 'cuz I got caught."

"Who caught you?"

"My ol' girl caught me." His father did not live with the rest of the family.

"What did your mother do?"

"First she flushed it down the toilet and then called the police on me. They took me down to the station, and they gave me a juvenile parole officer an' stuff."

"Are you going to sell again?"

"Ah, uh, yeah. My father said he used to do it; and he said if I'm going to do it, he wanted me to be careful."

"Yeah," interjected the first youth. "Same thing my mom said. [If I get caught] she's not comin' down to get me . . . wants me to learn a lesson." He added almost as an afterthought, "It's going to be my decision anyway. You're going to get six months anyway, if you get caught."

I asked an accomplished car thief how he managed to escape his mother's attention.

"I don't sneak out," he stated. "I just tell her that I'm going outside."

"You're fourteen years old, right? What time do you have to be home?"

"Nine-thirty."

"So all this stuff happens before ten?"

"Nah. Say I tell her I'm going to the skating rink and it's open until one o'clock. We go skating, then we go get the cars. I stay out all night, then tell my mother that I stayed over my friend's house."

"Does she know that you are making money doing this?"

"No."

"How do you keep it from her?"

"I go out and buy stuff, like gold. I tell her it's fake." He smiled and added, "You gotta survive, bro."

"Survival" was too strong a word to describe his motivation for lying to his mother, but it captured the exaggerated sense of intrigue and importance that youngsters such as he attributed to their own criminal behavior. Many need not have gone to such great lengths to hide what they were doing, if what a number of young men and women said to me was correct. As one young woman put it, "the kids will start bringin' the money in, and their parent will ask 'im where I get the money from. If there's somethin' [the parent] really wants and he's out of work, he's goin' to ask for the money to get it."

"Are you going to give it to him?"

"Yes. That way you can keep on bringin' it in, if you want."

"Is that typical?"

"As long as they get part of it. They try to tell us to stay out of trouble, but they still want the money."

"Any parents try to stop the kid?"

"Yeah. I've known parents to turn their kids in" (to the police).

"But most parents take the money?"

"Yeah."

"Do the kids talk about this a lot?"

"Yeah. They be comin' to school braggin' a lot ... 'My momma this ... my momma that.' Their momma know they don't work 'cause they too young to get a job. As long as they buy parents somethin', the parents let the money come in.

"Some parents try to discourage kids, don't they?"

"Sometimes they do ... 'cause there's a lotta stuff goin' on even in the neighborhood and stuff. People get shot. That's what really makes the parents want their kids to stop. I know some parents in my neighborhood, uh, they tried to form a little gang to keep their kids from sellin' drugs. They try to catch the big dealers with somethin', so they can turn them in."

"When the parents do accept the money, how much are we talking about?"

"Some people buy their parents cars ... or they may give them fifty dollars a day ..."

"Do the kids respect their parents when they give the parents money?"

"They say like their parents are real cool and stuff. 'They let me buy this.' It's like they sayin' she care, but she don't really care 'cause she let them do that."

"Do the children realize this?"

"No. They like it, 'cause they say their parents cool. You know other people start hangin' around because they like parents like that."

Young teens say their parents react to gang involvement in a variety of ways, and a small number of these boys and girls spoke in unflattering terms about the behavior of parents. Other youths were not at all concerned about the apparent willingness of their parents to let them engage in dangerous or illegal activities. Some parents sought to gain material advantages from their children's misdeeds.

If boys and girls in their early teens received different messages from their parents about gangs and drugs, they experienced no such confusion once they crossed the threshold of their homes and stepped on to the streets. The world of gangs became clearer for them out in the neighborhood. One was expected to show loyalty to his or her town and the gang representing it. Insofar as one's municipal gang was affiliated with a larger gang organization based in Los Angeles or Chicago, loyalty to the town gang or one's "hood" took precedence. Young persons in each town need not have become members in either a communal or a non-local gang. Indeed, most of them did not become members of any gang. Recognition and respect for gangs were anticipated, however, and most individuals willingly acceded to this state of affairs.

It took some time for me to tease out the relative importance of young people's town and non-local gang memberships. One youth captured much of what I had heard from a number of teenagers. "The city comes first," he observed. "Then comes the colors." The Crips and Bloods were identified by the colors they wore, blue for Crips and red for Bloods. "The city fighting the city?" he added. "That's been goin' on for I don't know how long. It started when my older brother was in junior high school. There wasn't no gang stuff until these wannabes and guys from California came."

This young man was one of several whom I interviewed who referred to "gangs" only in the context of the California Crips and Bloods. Most other teens identified the local groups as gangs as well. The transformation of a local gang into an affiliate of one or another "national organization" was neither mysterious nor difficult, as one young man helped me to understand.

"How did Vista Village go Blood?" I asked.

"It's like, okay, everybody in the hood is all friends with each others. And let's say like if your friend turn Blood, and you've been his friend ever since you been young, you went to jail with 'im and helped him fight and all that, so we're going to turn Blood with him. So it's like that."

"Are you going to buy your drugs from Crips?"

"Not really. But they will sell to Crips, because the money comes first. They're more into money than the gang stuff."

"Then why are the colors important?"

"Because it's like tradition, like . . . uh, five years ago my brother was doing a gang. Five years later I'm doin' it and passin' it down the line."

"So what's more important, the hood or the color?"

"The hood. Because before everybody was joining gangs, they was just known as Vista Village. It's like that."

"Were they a gang before becoming aligned with the Bloods?"

"Uh huh. Just a group."

"Did they do the same things as a 'group' that they did when they were a 'gang'?"

"Well yeah, just about. But with colors."

"Did they sell drugs?"

"Some did."

"Did they fight?"

"Yeah. Most definitely fightin'."

"And they had a territory and hung around together, right?"

"Right."

"So the only thing that really changed . . .?"

"Was the colors."

There were occasions when one's loyalties could pull a person in different directions. The responsibility to honor one's colors could conflict with his allegiance to a town. The two largest towns in the Fairview School District, Oakdale and Pine Ridge, had sections allied with the Crips and Bloods. This might have caused problems when teens from both towns had serious disagreements or fought, as they often did. After all, a Blood from Oakdale might have been put in the position of having to fight a Blood from Pine Ridge. It was just such occasions, however, that made clear just how important the loyalty to one's town and friends really was.

"Your first loyalty," I inquired of one youth, "is to the hood then, right?"

He nodded his head. "Oakdale Crips will fight Pine Ridge Crips," he said. In fact, everybody under the Crips from different towns would fight Oakdale, and they would even fight Crips from Oakdale.

"So the groups under different colors really haven't come together all that much, have they?"

"No they haven't."

"So there's not much loyalty under the Blood banner?"

He nodded his head in agreement.

"The banner matters more for drug dealing?"

"Right." He added that the only other time that one's colors mattered was in public places such as the skating rink when Crips and Bloods would fight each other. It did not matter where one was from on such occasions.

"That's when the colors fall together?"

"Right."

"Otherwise, it's the town loyalty that matters more?"

"Right."

A number of other teens confirmed this basic arrangement. They did not allow their "colors" to interfere with loyalty to their "hood."

I asked one youth which was more important and he replied, "Where you live, definitely." He added that town loyalty mattered more "like when somebody come walkin' into your neighborhood." The colors were more important "like when you go to the skatin' rink and walkin' around." He paused for a moment and then concluded by saying that colors mattered more for drug sales as well.

Finally, one fifteen-year-old who had lived his entire life in Pine Ridge told me that "you have the Pine Ridge Organization which covers everybody."

"But some are going to be Bloods and some are Crips," I noted. "How do they handle that?"

He explained that they just claimed membership in the broader township and did not bother each other. "The Bloods can walk anywhere they like in Pine Ridge. The Crips just keep to theyselves in their little spot. If they get to talkin' to each other, they'll help fight if someone try to take Pine Ridge over. Then they help each other . . . but they won't help each other jump no Crip or Blood. You gotta realize that PRO (Pine Ridge Organization) ain't a gang. It's another name for Pine Ridge."

That may have been true for the Crips and Bloods in Pine Ridge and Oakdale, the two large municipalities in the Fairview School District. In virtually all the smaller towns, however, the members of the communal gangs identified either with the Bloods or the Crips. The identification with one's town gang usually was stronger, and the occasions when it was not were well understood by all the young men and women with whom I spoke.

Other aspects of being a gang member were not as well understood. Some young men and women had more intimate knowledge of gang routines, because they were deeply involved with their particular group. Other teens who were not so deeply involved possessed less information about the organization and actions of their own gang and other gangs.

One thirteen-year-old named Derrick explained what it was like being on the periphery of his gang. "Me and a couple of friends . . . are not in the heart of it," he said. "We're their friends."

"Are these other boys who aren't 'in the heart of it' also white?"

Derrick nodded his head. "Some of 'em. A couple. Not too many."

"How did you come to be on the outside of it?"

"They just asked if I wanted to join and I said, 'Yeah sure.' We just do ordinary kid stuff. We don't go around breakin' windows or anything like that. We don't do drugs. We just hang out and have fun and stuff like that. Some may break off a car mirror, but they don't do heavy stuff like drugs. They may spray paint a sign. That's about it."

"Might some kids more deeply involved in your gang be selling drugs and you not know about it?"

"Probably. There's a lot of drugs on the street. You see we [peripheral members] don't get into the heavy stuff . . . only the inside group does."

"How many are in the, 'inside group'?"

"About twenty-three, maybe twenty-four."

"How about in the 'outside group' like you?"

"About maybe fifteen, twenty. I'm not sure."

"When the heart of the group goes out to fight another gang do you join them?"

"No. We don't have to. But if we want to, we can."

"Do the parents of kids like you know that their kid's in it?"

"Probably not."

"Does your mom know?"

"No."

"What would she do, if she did know?"

"If we had a bad reputation, then she would mind a lot."

"Are you known to be a gang member at school?"

"Not really. Just the main kids are known."

"Do you help them when they fight in the school?"

"No ... no outside people have jumped in so far."

"Do other black kids bother you because you're white?"

"No. But we had a couple of white kids get hit in the back of their heads. But that was because of the Ku Klux Klan business out at the Monroe High School in the city. The black kids want to make this an all-black school. They already drove out one white kid."

"What happened to him?"

"His mom's teaching him at home. His parents were afraid that he was going to be hurt."

"Have you ever been hit in the head?"

"Twice."

"Did you do anything about it?"

"Nothing really, because you don't want to go messin' with people in this school. They'll know bigger people, and them people will know even more people. And soon you could have most of the school on you."

He did not feel nearly so vulnerable out on the streets. If nothing else, there was always somewhere to run. It was different in school, particularly at Fairview Junior High School. There were hundreds of youngsters, but only a few dozen of them were white. Whatever anonymity they enjoyed in their community was absent here. They had no place to hide, and there were many black teenagers who seemed to need little excuse to start a fight.

This young man's experience was shared by other white teenagers. One girl recalled a conversation in which a white male was charged ten dollars by a black youth for the privilege of being left alone. Another white male said that he had been bothered by black students pretty regularly. "I've been approached twice to buy drugs," he said. "The first time a kid came up and wanted to sell me a bag of weed for eight dollars. The second time it was crack." On another occasion, he was invited to become a member of a gang.

"We have a lot of fun," he was told. When he asked what "fun" they had in mind, he was told, "stealing cars, selling drugs."

Yet a third white boy said that he no longer was afraid to walk in the school. He had been afraid after being hit. "You know, like the first three or four days after," he recalled. "But now I look behind me to see if anybody's coming up with a padlock to hit me. Other than that, no, I'm not afraid. I was hoping to make it through without being hit. But, oh well."

He was not alone. A number of young men and women, both black and white, expressed similar sentiments during my conversation with them. It apparently was difficult to mind one's own business at the junior high school.

"Most of the time up here," a young black woman told me, "it seem like the bigger kids they be walkin' down the hallway and be expectin' to get respect. They expect you to move. And if they ask you for somethin', they expect you to give it to 'em."

"What might they ask for?" I asked.

"Like your lunch. They'll ask you, 'Can I have some of this?' Then they'll just build it up . . . and then they want to fight you." The requests, or "hasslin' " as another student put it, for hats, jackets, and shoes were just an excuse for trying to start a fight.

"The girls and boys be takin' jackets. One side take a jacket, and we asked her to give it back. She didn't. So, we fought. It didn't have to happen. She said she didn't have it. But after the fight, her mother brought it up here. She had it at home."

While such episodes could involve any youngster at the school, a young woman told me that gang members were the most likely participants. "You could be the type that don't say nothin', but they'll think you scared." Then they'll say something to you. "It's a lot of "he-say she-say' bullshit. That's how all of it starts. They make up somethin' to say just to fight you. I feel it's the girl's fault, because they'll say somethin' about each other's boyfriend . . . silly stuff." The girls, she assured me, were quicker to react to such challenges. "The boys don't trip on that kinda stuff unless they hear it for theyselves."

Intimidation of students by their peers was viewed as an important source of friction in the nearly continuous disputes that seemed to exist between one or another gang represented at the school. Different groups seemed to take turns being the most provocative and obnoxious, but there was an undercurrent of ill-feeling between youngsters from Oakdale and Pine Ridge that never seemed to wane. As the largest municipalities in the district, they provided more potential combatants to the mix of students at the school.

How much conflict occurred between any two gangs at the school depended a great deal on how many of their members were in attendance and the current state of their relations outside of school. I asked one member of the Rose Terrace gang why young men from Vista Village wanted to fight his group. "Because, well, like they want to come up here actin' like Bloods," he said. "Well really we tight with Bloods ... so just tol' 'em we'd be Crips." They pretended to be something they were not just so that they could fight the Rose Terrace gang.

"When will the fighting begin?"

"I don't know. One of 'em will come up to you and say somethin' that you don't really agree with or somethin' like that. And then he'll go back and get his brother and then ... they'll get some of everybody, and they just come up here."

"What will happen, if their leader isn't at school?"

"They'll feel uncomfortable ... Right. It's like if there's a couple of us standin' out in the hall talkin' to each other an' they leader ain't there, and they all know it. They'll walk down the hall talkin' a whole bunch of stuff, sayin' they gonna beat somebody down and all that. And we gonna go up to 'um and tell 'um you're boys ain't here. He'll get scared and run out through the side door or somethin' like that." Sometimes the intended targets do not even bother to come to schools because they are afraid.

"So when does it start?" I inquired.

"Well ... it's mainly ... you got some [gang members] up at the high school. They be fightin' up there, then it will carry back down here. They'll wait 'til we get to walkin' down towards they way ... 'cuz we want to mess with some girls or somethin' ... It's like they'll chase us. Once ... some people got shot at."

"Do you know who did it? Does he go to this school?"

"He'll go to school a couple of days, and he'll come back when he thinks his boys here. But mainly he got ... [friends] and they're always walkin' him to school and standin' up there on the corner [waiting to see what happens]. If you find out that he's in school, then you got kids up here who do research ... [find] out where their classes are at. And whatever happens does happen."

What usually "happens" is a fight. What usually does not "happen" is effective adult intervention before, during, or after the fight. That is why the prospective victim thought it necessary to have his mates serve as a substitute mother and walk him safely to school. The adults at the school did little or nothing to end the cycle of intimidation and violence among their students. By virtue of the staff's inattentiveness, what took place in the school accentuated the bad feelings that students held for each other and fueled ongoing disputes between rival groups.

Part of the explanation for this situation could be attributed to the way public schools were organized. The junior high school was the first setting where youngsters from all municipalities and gangs had regular access to each other. They took advantage of this fact and carried whatever disagreements they might have been having on the streets into the school. My conversations with school staff and students convinced me, however, that lingering animosity between youngsters from different towns would have persisted no matter what the adults who ostensibly ran the school had done.

The reaction of the adults to these ongoing disputes would not have made ill-feelings go away. Nevertheless, disagreements could have been tempered and the amount of friction at the school could have been reduced. The behavior of school staff actually nurtured these disputes by failing to recognize how fights originated. They did not perceive much, if any, group or gang influence in these episodes. They preferred to view each new incident as a novel event and the rule breakers as individual troublemakers who could be handled most effectively by tossing them out of school for shorter or longer periods of time, depending on the gravity of their offense.

While school staff knew that many fights occurred over articles of clothing or "he-say she-say" stuff, they failed to put these events into a larger context. It was "just another fight between kids from different towns." There was a constant stream of students in and out of the vice principals' offices. Students were routinely suspended for one or another violation, but that was the extent of any "policy" regarding these ongoing disputes. School staff made a practice of tolerating brawls and gang fights. In so doing, they provided an environment conducive to broader gang activity in the school.

There were teachers or security guards posted at major intersections of the school's corridors when students were moving from one to another class. This did not stop fights from occurring. Indeed, a number of students commented on the unwillingness of staff to stop students from fighting. As one young man said, "You got some teachers who just sit there and watch. And once they see somebody gettin' beat up too bad, then that's when they'll go to stop it. You really wouldn't hear about no teacher try to break it up. They'll wait 'til it's almost finished with."

I witnessed one of these episodes and observed no active intervention by school staff until the fight had nearly ended. Some classroom doors were closed at the time, but teachers were in attendance during the fracas and no doubt could hear the noise outside of their rooms. Numerous students expressed disdain for the behavior of their peers and adult supervisors after these outbursts. This included students who were not in gangs but were willing to act as they saw others behave in order to protect themselves in this environment.

One young woman told me that the presence of gangs in the school bothered her, "because you can be hurt anytime." She added that the school's two security guards would "rather stand out of the way . . . [when] Oakdale and Pine Ridge fight, and all the police have to come up here. It's ridiculous."

I noted that there were a lot of students who were not involved and asked her whether they were frightened when there were fights after school.

"Sometimes," she said, "if there's goin' to be a gun, they'll get on the bus and go home. If it's just a fistfight, they'll stay and watch."

"Have you been afraid?"

"Yes," she replied.

"Why?"

" 'Cuz, okay, if one person do somethin' to another person, they friend will go out and get all them gang members and jump on that one person. One girl tried to do that to me, but I got ready for her. I told all my friends."

"Have you fought yet?"

She shook her head. "We almost did in the classroom."

"Is this girl in a gang?"

"Nope."

"How did it start?"

"She said something to me and said she was jokin', but I took it seriously. I told the girl, 'You start it. I'll end it. No problem.' "

"Do you kids ever talk among yourselves about stopping this gang stuff at school?"

"Sometimes. We say we wish we could put all the bad people in jail. They have been talked to a lotta times. Instead of doin' somethin' bad to hurt somebody, they should try to think of somethin' good to make them respect theyself."

"A lot of students feel this way?"

"I only tell this to my one good friend and some other kids. The fighting and drug dealing bothers them. People go out and get on crack, and then you want to go to college and be the best that you can be. But you have a jail record . . . and you can't keep your mind on anything because your head's all filled with drugs. That ain't the way to go."

"How do you stay out of it?"

"I just don't hang with certain people. You gotta hang with your own crowd, or else you end up just like the gang members."

"But aren't the gang kids more popular?"

"Yes," she noted strongly. " 'Cuz they got gold chains and funky clothes and all."

"And aren't they more sexually active?"

"Yes. 'Cuz once you get popular it seems that every girl wants to sleep with 'em. They think he's so popular that if they do it with him, they can spread it all over school."

"The girls take this as a point of pride?"

She nodded her head. "And then they get popular. They name stands out. Everybody know 'em. Everybody like praise them and all."

"What do you think of that?"

"I think it's stupid. Being popular ain't nothin'. I be just like me. I be doin' fine, and I ain't fuckin'. I'm doin' my grades right. I got nothin' to worry about. I just go to college and get my education, and my job, and live in good health."

"And finish any unwanted business brought your way in the meantime?"

She looked calmly into my eyes and said, "Right."

I nodded. "Definitely not someone to mess with," I thought to myself.

Gangs occupied a prominent spot in the social hierarchy of the junior high school. They entered the school with considerable credibility and clout in the eyes of most students. They reinforced their position by intimidating each other's members and students who were not aligned with them. Still, it was the abrogation by adults of their own authority that made the gangs so effective. Staff failed to stop fights or even to address seriously the root causes of fights between "kids from different towns." In words that gang members themselves might have used, the adults "punked."

I have no doubt that town rivalries would have persisted and tempers continue to flare up had there been no gangs at Fairview Junior High School. Yet it was gang members who were the primary instigators of fights at the school. Their petty disagreements and animosities fueled disputes, made credible the putative threats to their sovereignty, and kept most everyone anxious.

Gang rivalries and fights were the most obvious expression of trouble at the school. Students were preoccupied with the most up-to-date gossip on which groups were likely to fight or who was next in line to be jumped, and school staff were kept busy tidying up after the last fight or assault. Another activity sponsored almost exclusively by gangs in the school was drug dealing. While it involved only a small portion of the teens who allied themselves with gangs, drug dealing had a more corrosive effect on the school. Really big fights might provoke a police response, but fights of such magnitude generally occurred after school as students were going home. In general, fighting was accepted as a "normal" part of the school's routine and just something that teenagers did.

Drug dealing, on the other hand, clearly was illegal. Yet it received even less attention from school staff than did fighting. The sale of marijuana, different types of pills, or crack cocaine and the ingestion of some of these substances as well as alcohol were openly acknowledged by a great many students. Adults did not react to such behavior as if it were a serious problem, much less a threat to the health and well-being of the students or school. Drugs were Fairview Junior High School's dirty little secret.

"Is there any drug dealing at this school?" I asked one young woman.

"Do I have to say?" she inquired.

"No, you don't have to say," I replied. "But you know I don't want any kid's name."

She nodded her head. "Yeah, I guess you might say so. Nothin' like crack or ice or anything like that."

"What is it then?"

"It's mostly, you know, speed. They might try to sell you some heart pills and stuff."

"Are these kids in gangs?"

"Mostly. Some of them are independents."

"How many kids sell this stuff?"

"Most of them."

"White or black kids?"

"Mostly black ... I'll see kids giving money and receive stuff."

"Does this bother you?"

She pulled on her long brown hair and said, "As long as I'm not doin' it, I don't care."

One teenage boy related a conversation that he had with a second youth, while they were spending time in a class for students being punished for one transgression or another. "I was in in-school suspension," he said, "and I asked him if he had any money. He said, 'Ya, I brung some stones to school yesterday.' And he said he knocked them off at school. So, I guess he's selling them to students."

Another youth observed that some dealers "have someone come up to school at the door."

"You mean while classes are going on?"

He nodded his head. "You will meet them at the door. You'll skip class and meet them at the door. They do a little talkin', and then they trade ... money for drugs."

I was puzzled that this could happen. "Surely the teachers know?" I asked.

He nodded his head again. "The dealers wear those big gold chains, and they have beepers that go off in the classroom. They stop what they're doing and ask for a pass. I guess they're goin' to the pay phone on the first floor." He added that he knew of one student who was suspended for doing this.

One young man who admitted to selling drugs while at school said that he knew of ten or eleven kids who also were dealing at the school. "They do it during class ... in the rest room." He knew of only five students who used drugs on a typical school day and another six who became drunk on liquor brought into school in "little bottles." He had never been caught selling drugs. He and other students did not think many students were caught selling or ingesting drugs.

Another teenager conceded that he had been stopped by school staff. "They suspected me of sellin' drugs," he said, "because I keep a lot of money ... on me. One day I came in and they brought me to the office ... made me empty my pockets ... started checkin' me to see if I had drugs. Somebody told 'em I had four rocks on me."

"Did you?"

"Not that day," he replied. "The only reason that I bring 'em is because I was goin' somewhere to sell 'em right after school. I go down to the southside [of the city] and take maybe five of 'em with me. Others of my friends go to other places."

"Is there much selling that goes on in the school?"

"There is quite a bit of sellin' that goes on here during the day," he answered.

"Do different gangs have their own territories inside the school? Places where only they can hang out or sell drugs?"

"In the lunch-room there are certain tables," he noted, "that are Bloods' tables and Crips' tables."

"And just they sit at those tables?"

"Yeeeh. Everybody knows who sits at these tables every day."

"Any other parts of school that 'belong' to specific groups?"

"It's like this," he said. "You know the third floor bathroom?"

"Yes," I replied.

"That's the bathroom where everybody does the drinkin', because you can get away with anything up there. A principal is not going to go up three flights of stairs to use the rest room." Other students noted that the bathrooms also were used by persons smoking marijuana.

Most students when asked how many of their peers sold drugs at school had knowledge of five or fewer such persons. This was not surprising, given the illegal and secretive nature of the trade. Even those who had no firsthand information about drug dealing, however, were aware nonetheless that sales were being made.

One young woman told me how boys "talk about it with their friends and stuff," and tell people about selling "rocks and marijuana." She knew "about ten who use marijuana at school during the day. There's one person I know," she added, "every day he asks the teacher can he go to the bathroom. Everybody knows what he's doin' in there. Mrs Smith always says 'Yeah.'"

"And he comes back 'stoned'?"

"Yeah."

"Do the teachers know?"

"I think they know, but they pretend that they don't." A few students were astute enough to realize that those who were "stoned" ordinarily put their heads on their desk and were no trouble to the teacher. This young woman, however, could not move beyond her disapproval for the student's and teacher's behavior.

She believed the teacher to be wrong in letting him do that: "I think

they should do something about it. They should never let him go to
the bathroom. Last year we had a problem with the boys' bathroom.
It smelled just like marijuana. You open that door, and they just be smokey
in there."

Some teachers, several teens noted, did not accept into their classroom
students who were "bent" on alcohol or marijuana. "They give you a green
slip and send you down to the principal, if they think you're usin'." The
students sent to the principal's office were punished, as far as their peers
knew.

One young man recalled how he had been suspended for three days for
bringing beer into the school. "If the teacher notices it, the next day the
kid won't be there," he said. "It seemed like they're turned in, but no one
knows about it except the teacher, the kid, and the principal."

I do not know how many teachers ignored students who were under the
influence of some drug. Nor do I know how many teachers referred such
students to school administrators for disciplinary action. I do know that
teachers who did nothing made a big impression on students.

I found it interesting that no student had anything nice to say about any
of his or her teachers. I was not surprised that young men or women who
were affiliated with gangs had little or nothing good to say about the school
staff; but I had expected some of the so-called "good kids" to say something
of a positive nature. I was wrong.

I heard more conversations in which teachers were portrayed as uncaring
and incompetent. A young woman noted how one of her teachers just sat
at her desk and combed her hair. "They should check these people out before
they hire them," she argued. "She'll just tell you to read your book. The
whole class will sit there during a test with their books open. The whole
class! She's just sitting up there putting in her contacts. She turns around
and sees the books but doesn't say anything. I have a math teacher who
grades our homework during the class."

Another teenage girl said she knew of three teachers who were drunk or
stoned during the day. "One's a new teacher. We've been knowin' since
she got here from the smell and the way she act. There's another one, too.
The whole class knows it. They think we should go to the principal and
tell on her to get her fired. The two new teachers drink together. It's all
over the school."

If word of inappropriate conduct on the part of teachers had spread "all
over the school" as the young woman indicated, one might have thought
it unnecessary to bring the information to the attention of the principal.
After spending nearly a month in this school, I suspected that the principal
might be the last person to hear anything about everything. I saw him only
twice during the course of my visits to the school. A number of students
told me that sightings of the principal were sometimes separated by a month

or longer. This was confirmed by several staff with whom I conversed informally.

It is important to note that these were individuals who actually knew what the principal looked like. When most students said that they were going to meet "the principal," they were referring to one of several vice principals who had routine contact with them and were the school's chief disciplinarians. They did not know who the principal was. They could not tell me his name.

I first met the principal at a meeting in the superintendent's conference room. I was being introduced to all of the district's principals. The man who was identified as the junior high school principal did not look imposing and said nothing during the hour-long meeting. Several of his colleagues either asked me questions or commented – some favorably, some not – about the project that I was going to undertake. I thought at the time that junior high students would "eat this guy alive." The truth is that they did not even need to try.

I was told that he was popular with his staff, in part because he left them alone to do their jobs and was willing to suspend students who caused trouble or broke rules. He also was said to write good memos and have cordial relations with members of the Board of Education. He had been principal of the junior high school for over a decade, and he seemed to be in no danger of losing that job to someone else.

I had my only private meeting with him on the day that I began interviewing students in his school. It was a civil occasion. He sat behind his desk. I sat across from him. He seemed ill at ease. I admired the cleanest desk top, scuff and dust-free linoleum floor, and antiseptic office space into which I had ever set foot. He asked a little question or two. I provided little answers and wondered if anything ever had been dropped on his floor. The whole affair was over in ten minutes.

I saw him on only one other occasion while I was in the school, but it was a memorable moment. My sighting occurred one afternoon near the end of my stay. I had received a number of comments from students about his phantasmic administrative style. Perhaps more out of a sense of boredom than a desire to be a good scientist, I decided to see just how smooth an operation he ran and whether I might draw him from his lair. I mentioned to one of the vice principals my surprise at not seeing the principal around the school. I quickly added my hope that his apparent absence was not due to some illness. That said, I turned and beckoned the student waiting for me to join me in the conference room across the hallway.

We were about five minutes into the interview when someone knocked on the door to the conference room. I halted the interview and invited whoever was out there to come in. The door opened, and in stepped the principal. He was most apologetic, but he explained that he needed to take a chair from the room for a meeting that was being held down the hall. He picked up a chair and quietly left the room.

I could not enjoy the moment. It had been too easy.

"Why you shaking your head?" asked the student. "Somethin' wrong?"

I looked at him, smiled slightly, and said, "Nothing that won't pass."

Note

1 Felix M. Padilla, *The Gang as an American Enterprise* (New Brunswick, NJ: Rutgers University Press, 1992).

4

Going Along with the Program

School Daze

Dwayne Turner was the principal of Fairview High School. A tall and sturdily built black man who favored neatly tailored suits and steady habits, Mr Turner imagined that this would be the last administrative job in a career that had taken him through a variety of posts in several school districts. He had seen a great deal in his years as a teacher and principal. All of it, the good and the bad, had tested him and made him certain of who he was and what he could accomplish.

Fairview High School was a large school, but not the toughest duty he had ever drawn. "The sixties," he said while turning his eyes upward and shaking his head gently, "were something else. Student protests, riots, school strikes." Still, he knew that being the principal of a virtually all-black high school, with a tired and less than stellar faculty, in a nearly insolvent school district would offer him some special challenges. He had not been disappointed.

The school he had inherited only a few years earlier was by all accounts a mess. He walked in and tried to restore a sense of order to school routines and civility to the conduct of its students. His superiors thought that he had made progress. His students respected what he was trying to do and how he went about the business of running the school.

Dwayne Turner worked with his students. He was mindful of their shortcomings, but he respected what they could accomplish with hard work and diligence. He had that personal quality we sometimes refer to as "presence." It was an attitude that he projected as an administrator and as a man. He seemed in all ways but one to be the very antithesis of his counterpart at the junior high school. Dwayne Turner did not believe that his school had a gang presence, much less a gang problem.

He made this clear during our first conversation at the high school. I reviewed the progress of my project up to that point and we discussed the current situation at the high school. While he acknowledged that youngsters from different towns sometimes fought and expressed ill-feeling toward each other, he believed that tension at the school had been reduced and whatever problems they experienced were greatly overstated in the local press. He expressed no opinion about my assessment of conditions at the junior high school, but he clearly was not surprised by the tenor and content of my observations. Whatever might be occurring at the junior high school, he assured me that gangs were not a problem at his school.

I asked him what he thought about the group of young men standing just outside the window of his office. Mr Turner occupied the corner office on the ground floor of a building that looked out on to a quadrangle. Students crossed the quadrangle in order to reach one of four buildings that were the heart of the high school's campus. During our conversation the group of five or six young men to which I had drawn Mr Turner's attention had been standing at the entrance to the cafeteria, a building contiguous to the one we occupied.

I had watched this group as Mr Turner spoke with me. The students were no more than thirty feet from where we sat, and the principal saw them clearly once he turned his chair to the right. He watched them for a few moments and then turned to me. I repeated my question: "Well, what do you think?"

I do not recall precisely what he said, but it was obvious that he attributed no special significance to the group. I offered a summary of my observations over the previous fifteen or twenty minutes. I noted the color of their clothing. (Most of it was blue.) I described their demeanor. (They filled that space near the cafeteria entrance with the same sense of proprietorship that the principal had expressed when he filled the walls of his office with photographs and plaques.) I provided an account of the stylized greetings they offered some young men dressed like themselves and made particular reference to the hand gestures that they seemed to employ. In response to everything I said, Mr Turner struck a pose of studied indifference. There was nothing remarkable about this group as far as he was concerned.

(His attitude was all the more surprising, given his uncritical acceptance some weeks later of my report that a group of his students, whom I identified to him one afternoon while sitting in his office, were practicing satanists. "They're workin' on puppy dogs, pussy cats," one of his students had stated, while cringing. Mr Turner said he was not surprised.)

I elected not to push my point about the gang members standing just outside of his office, and he offered no elaboration of his position. In the space of that brief exchange, we had come to a quick and cordial understanding about gangs in his school. I was free to see them. He was free to deny their significance. There was no need to speak further about that particular matter.

We did speak briefly about the size and composition of the list of students whose names appeared as interview subjects. He already knew that I had interviewed over a hundred students at the junior high school. There was no question that the list of two dozen or so names he had presented to me would grow as I met with students. And yes, of course, I would bring to his attention any fight or serious problem that seemed to be in imminent danger of breaking out, just as long as he understood that I would not share the name of the youngster who had given me the information. Our meeting completed, we both rose and shook hands. The deal was cut. I was in.

Once outside his office, I was introduced to his secretary. Mr Turner waited long enough to hear me request the first name from his list. He was visibly surprised when I requested someone whose name was not on the list, particularly so, I imagined, because the young woman probably would have been among the least likely persons at the school to have any firsthand experience with gangs. Natalie Brown was a bright, quiet, and well-mannered teenager. She would be attending college in the fall, and she had virtually no knowledge about gangs. As she was the daughter of a friend I had already been able to ascertain this, but Mr Turner did not know about my relationship with this student and her family. The look of bewilderment was still on his face when Natalie entered the office and walked with me to where the interview would be conducted.

Even if Natalie had told me nothing useful, it would have been worth the time just to see Mr Turner's face when my first interview was with someone who probably never used profanity much less hung around with gangbangers. However, Natalie was a useful subject because she helped me to understand the extent to which gangs influenced the school's daily routine or other students who were not gang members. I learned from her that gangs at the high school were a great deal different from gangs at the junior high.

"I don't know of particular gangs," she said. "I just know of friends who stick together, who hang around with each other. They get into arguments . . . I don't know how the fights start . . . as far as gangs go. Most of the time, the fights . . . are based upon where you live."

"How often do fights occur?" I asked.

"It's gotten a little better. The majority of the fights are by individuals, but a lot of times, like once or twice a week, it might be a group of people."

"What do kids say about these fights afterward?"

"They say somebody jumped on one of them with more than one

friend . . . when they were alone. They start in the cafeteria a lot of the time, or on the quadrangle, or on the first floor of a building." These were the most heavily travelled parts of the school, places where large numbers of youngsters from different towns were more likely to bump into each other.

"What do students who aren't involved in these fights think?"

"They usually say, 'Well if you just walk away and don't pay any attention to 'em, then they won't fight, because they're only doing it for attention.' Like I say, it's just an ongoing thing. A lotta times they don't even have a good reason. It can be something like, 'Well he stepped on my shoe.' But it goes back to another time when they all jumped on him."

"Do you try to do anything about the fights?"

Natalie replied that there was "not too much you can do, 'cuz you can't go into a fight and try to stop it. So, I just try to walk away."

"Do teachers try to stop it?"

"They do."

"Are they successful?"

"They have to have the guards to help. I guess you'd have to say that it works sometimes and sometimes it doesn't. Sometimes a teacher can't stop a whole fight. If you intervene, then you get involved, too. It starts in the neighborhoods, and they bring it into the school. I don't think a lot of the problems start in the school."

"Are the girls different?" I asked.

"Most of the time the girls fight one-on-one, whereas the boys go in groups. With the girls it's not the neighborhood. It can be over a boy. To me it does not make any sense."

"Do they use weapons?"

"Usually they just use their hands. Sometimes a weapon, a knife." She also had heard about a gun having been brought to school one time.

"Any drug dealing on campus?"

"I have not heard one thing about it. I've heard people talking about it in classes. People say you can get it anywhere."

"Do people come to school drunk?"

"I've never seen anyone drinking, but sometimes you can smell it on their breath. That's only happened once or twice."

"Is there anything about this school that you don't like?"

"It's predominantly black. I like that part. But they all fight each other. They egg each other on. If more people just walked away, there'd be less fighting. They act like little creeps. Each group wants to be on top."

Insofar as Fairview High School had gangs, they were an embarrassment and nuisance for Natalie. The fights that she witnessed disrupted the school day, but they did not seem to have interrupted her education to the point that she considered the time spent in school wasted.

A teenage boy shared this attitude. It wasn't really hard to stay out of trouble with the gangs, he said. "If you come up here and look for an education, they won't mess with you. If you mind your own business, you're all right. It's not like you come to Fairview and you're goin' to have a fight."

"But there's trouble here, if you look for it?" I asked.

"There's trouble to be found anywhere, if you look for it. We have a bad reputation because things get spread that are not true."

Another male student suggested that the school's main problems were "too many students and not enough money. The reputation that's been poured on us so graciously has had an impact. When you come here you expect to see, uh, total chaos. Guns and knives, which I haven't seen any of. But you hear it. So I guess people come here and try to lower their morals and self-esteem so they fit in."

"Is that why you needed a group like A Few Good Men?"

"He nodded his head in agreement. "The lack of positive role models . . . who can show these itty-bitty boys with no morals how they should be."

"Has it worked, despite being around for only a few months?"

"Yes! Yes it has. You can see it most in the younger students . . . in the way they act. You know. The cussin' in the halls. Little petty things like that. A Few Good Men will go up to them and say, 'Why do you do that?' or 'Take your hat off.' or 'Why don't you pick up your lunch tray?'"

"So the edges around here have become less rough?" I inquired.

"A little bit," he replied. "It will get better."

"Are the over-aged kids a big problem?"

"Yes. Yes."

"They make themselves noticeable by doin' nothing. Lounge around. Look negative."

"Do many students try to emulate them?"

"Yes. I think so." He paused, as if to choose his next words carefully. "It seems to me," he continued, "that there's a problem with them. [They] should not be here. It seems like they have no penalties. They get to do whatever they like."

"Such as?"

"They fight a lot. Okay. They're back in two days. Have another fight? They're back in a week. It's just repetitive. I think they should be out . . . after a certain amount of times doing things. It's shocking to me that it works the way it does. It's very upsetting to people who want to do better and have a positive attitude. The bad ones should be booted out."

"Do other students share this view?"

"Yes."

"Do the over-aged troublemakers make a point of intimidating students who would be more positive?"

"No. I've never seen that. They intimidate the ones who can be intimidated."

"Do teachers ignore disciplinary problems?"

He did not think so; but he was certain that these students had an impact on the classroom. "Some teachers," he observed, "concentrate more on discipline than on the work. There are a lot of times when teachers spend a whole class period arguing with some kid who showed up late rather than dealing with the material. There are teachers who'd rather come in and say, 'Here's the work sheet. Go ahead.' There are a lot of teachers really not doing their job."

A female senior was equally certain that gangs had hurt her high school education. "I came into high school with kinda high expectations," she said, "but they kinda got trampled down because, you know, these gangs runnin' around. They have you trapped in the midst of all this, because they attend the school we do. You are subject to the rules ... put out ... because of them. It's like we're limited because of them." She cited the rule prohibiting students from leaving the campus for lunch as a small example of how "good kids" were punished because of the way "bad kids" behaved.

"Do you know who the gang members are?"

"I have no idea ... I don't stop to watch the fights."

"Do other kids watch the fights?"

"They run to them." She noted in passing that the "number of fights has been decreasing. All of the fights aren't gang related, but the majority of them are, I'd say."

A young black man told me about a confrontation he had on campus with a Blood. "He pulled a gun on me and my two friends ... last year ...' cuz we were playin' ball and his team lost. And he go, 'Yeeeh. You a punk. I got you a punk like that.' I said, 'Why don't you do somethin' about it.' Next thing ... he had his hand on his belt buckle. He pulls out his gun, and I look at him with a look that says, 'You shouldn't have did that.'"

He and his friends took the gun away from the gang member.

Another young man claimed that different parts of the cafeteria were occupied by specific gangs. "They had the Bloods and Crips fighting up here last January," he said, "and some people got hurt. Some guy throws a punch at me, and I said, 'You're mine.' The next thing I know, somebody else punched him out from the side. I looked down at him and said, 'I guess you wasn't mine,' and walked away."

This particular youth had been adopted by a white family. He and his half-brother were close, and this created some problems for him. Other blacks, he noted, said things like, "You a honkey lover."

He recalled standing his ground after once such exchange and saying, "Yeah. And I got two cars, a house, and I don't sell drugs, and I make my money legal. What can you do? You ain't got nothin' to show for yourself. So thank you."

"What happens then?" I inquired.

"Then I walk off. I have no trouble after that," he replied.

Students may have been able to avoid being drawn into a gang fight, but that did not insulate them from the effects of gang disputes. One teenager bemoaned the fact that so many boys were "tryin' to be like a Crip or Blood . . . wearin' blue or red rags. My friend says he's a Gangster Disciple. I tell him, 'You wear a blue rag around me and I'll kill ya. If I get shot at, I'm goin' to kill ya still. So keep the blue rag off. I don't wanna see no blue or red rag around me.' "

Another youth recalled how "one time this guy was in the parking lot. He said he was a Blood, and another kid said, 'You think that's Blood? I'll show you blood.' And he jumped on the Blood and took a big bite out of him. It was, ughh, disgusting . . . bit him like an animal. I don't know if the other young man was from this campus, but the very same day there was a large fight on the quadrangle. People said it was Crips and Bloods. For a while after that there were people who came to school dressed in blue and people who came dressed in red. But I never thought they were really true Crips or really true Bloods."

He and other students not affiliated with gangs believed that most of these fights could be traced back to rivalries between towns and the gangs that were found in most of these places. As one youth put it, "kids from different communities will get into it. They'll help someone from their own town. Nobody up here seems to believe in a one-on-one fight. It's always like, 'Well you hit him first.' Then I come in with my group."

Another young man said that the big fight at school just before Christmas had been noteworthy but not because anyone used a weapon. Rather, "it was big because it just moved from one part of the campus to another. A couple of people'd be fightin' and there'd be a crowd. The fight would move or have a couple more people get into it, and the crowd would move with them."

The rivalries between towns were taken for granted and usually treated as if they were "no big deal." Indeed, "most of the people up here don't fight. And those who fight . . . usually [are] the same bunch. It's not like groups of twenty people gettin' into it."

Others acknowledged that the kind of freewheeling and large group fights seen more frequently at the junior high school were not commonplace at the high school. At the same time, however, smaller group fights did occur regularly. "Possibly once a week with up to six guys on a side," one student said. Many students agreed with that observation.

They also agreed about the cause of most fights. It was not just drugs, one student noted. "Most of it's territorial, claimin' fame." Disagreements over drug distribution or sales outside of school simply reinforced gang rivalries and provided a reason for fights on campus.

Both boys and girls took part in these engagements, but for different reasons. "The girls who fight," as one student stated, "fight over jealousy and boys." Boys from the same town might fight, but most of the time fights occurred between young men from different towns. "But it's not like it's over drugs or anything. It's usually over somebody's cousin, you know, something really stupid. They don't use knives or guns. They use fists. It's like brothers that always have problems, they just fight over it. Fightin' is natural. It's like they live so close together that they fight. But it's nothing real drastic like people dying or anything."

Few students, however, made any reference to fighting as a "natural thing" that teenagers do. They were much more likely to make rather careful and well-articulated observations about the ritual or prescribed character of most fights. Virtually everyone who commented about fighting, for instance, noted that persons rarely used lethal weapons. It seemed to be a rule that most people followed closely. They also noted the infrequency with which really large gang fights occurred and persons were "jumped" by roving bands of miscreants.

Several students offered additional insights into the way fighting at the high school had become restrained or more limited than it had been at the junior high. There was some opinion that fighting was more likely to occur at the end of a school year. "Most people," as one student put it, "want to go out with a gang bang at the end of the year. They don't have to worry about comin' back to school or bein' seen. You can't be suspended or anything like that."

More prevalent was the observation that fighting occurred with greater frequency at the beginning of each school year. "I think there's a reason to it," one young man stated. "At the beginning of the year it was a freshman problem, because they had this reputation from the junior high. I think they had to come up here and show themselves, or give themselves a reputation that will last throughout the years."

"Did it work?" I asked.

"No."

"Would you expect it next year?"

"Yes . . . even more."

"Why?"

"I've been to the junior high school and seen the group that will be here next year."

"The ones who fight," another student maintained, "are the newcomers tryin' to make a name for themselves. The people who have been up here for a couple of years . . . they already know what's happenin'. They try to lay back, be cool."

Gangs and fighting at the high school were different, and there were several plausible explanations for why they would be different. The age and experience of gang members surely would be important factors. These individuals were older and, presumably, at least a little more sophisticated by the time they reached their third and fourth years at the high school. Most gang members did not find it necessary or think it advisable to be as loud, rowdy, or violent as they had once been. The older members no longer had a need to "show off" and make themselves an object of public attention and scrutiny. Insofar as it was necessary for a gang to make its presence felt, younger members could be counted on to do most of the work. Better established gang members did not even have to ask younger students to assume this responsibility. The young ones were eager to strike out on their own.

Much popular and scientific discussion about gangs and juvenile delinquency focuses generally on the age of would-be members and offenders as an important factor in predicting or explaining their behavior.[1] People remark that young men and women in their late teens or early twenties probably are less likely to commit delinquent or criminal acts than are boys and girls in their early teens. They simply "grow up" and become more mature. Indeed, the phenomenon of "maturing out" is well known among those of us who have studied gangs for any length of time. Individual gang members gradually assume more conventional adult roles and spend less time gangbanging. They become "old guys," gangbanger emeriti who offer advice and support but rarely take part in gang activities.

I do not doubt that there is some merit to this general line of reasoning. I have interviewed too many older gang members who shook their heads and dismissed as "stupid" the antics of their young associates to argue otherwise. At the same time, I do not think that this is either the most important or the most interesting explanation for why there were fewer big fights and less fighting generally at Fairview High School. The students in question were, after all, hardly a bunch of old geezers with pot bellies and bad teeth. They were young, strong, and, as their behavior on the street indicated, not at all adverse to "mixing it up" with their rivals or putative allies. Furthermore, we know from media reports and scholarly research that gang activity ordinarily peaks at the high school level. It does not drop off.

No one except the principal and a few of his Few Good Men argued that gangs were not a problem at Fairview High School. It would be inaccurate and unfair to say, however, that gangs disrupted many school routines, defied adult authority at every turn, and made life almost unbearable for the vast majority of students who were not gang members. A number of students indicated that one could go to classes and get something approximating an education and walk down the hallway without fear of being assaulted or recruited by gang members. Notwithstanding the fights between individuals and small groups, mediocre performance by teachers and students, and bad publicity, the school was not out of control. In fact, several administrators and a number of students believed that the situation was improving; and they attributed the school's modest turnaround to the hard work and steady hand of the principal, Dwayne Turner.

The personal example set by Mr Turner and the policies he was instrumental in introducing made Fairview High School a better place, but he did not rid the school of gangs or even greatly reduce their presence on campus. I was told by students that a number of gang members had been suspended from school, and that might have accounted for some of the reduction in overt gang activity. Yet gangs at the junior high school remained troublesome despite the constant stream of students sent to "the office" or being suspended for one or another violation of school rules. Moreover, there still were more than enough active gang members at the school to stage a good-sized row on the quadrangle or to supply different cafeteria tables with a full complement of gang members from each town. I saw only one such fight on the quadrangle during my visits to the school and had several opportunities to observe the posturing that took place in the cafeteria. So, too, did a police officer who was stationed in the cafeteria during each lunch period.

Gang members and their supporters could have been more disruptive had they chosen to be. Instead, they restrained themselves. The reason for this was related in part to their age and experience, but not in a way that could be tied to any hormonal readjustment or emotional awakening. It was rather that gang members had grown accustomed to the idea and fact of sharing the same school with persons they were not supposed to like. This realization had not come easily. They arrived as freshmen with a two-year apprenticeship from the junior high in school-based gangbanging, quick to take offense and willing to fight. Once at the high school, they were taught by their older peers not to take offense quite so quickly and not to fight as often or as recklessly as they had grown accustomed to doing at the junior high school.

Members of A Few Good Men had begun to contribute to this effort. They focused their attention on the younger students, which was a good idea. The example set by older gang members probably did a lot more, however, to curb the practice of instigating gang fights on a routine basis and to leave alone those who wanted nothing to do with gangs.

There simply was not as much intimidation and harassment of students at the high school. Everyone had come to understand that they had a legitimate claim to the school and whatever services were provided there, regardless of their hometown or gang affiliation. There was little or no graffiti on the walls of buildings; and youngsters congregated in large groups only during lunch periods, athletic events, and dances. It was on these occasions when one was more likely to hear groups calling out the names of their respective townships or throwing down challenges to students who were not in their gang. Otherwise, it was possible to walk unmolested to one's classes. Short of leaving school altogether or being tossed out permanently, the students knew that they would be with each other for four more years.

Many students may have failed to take full advantage of the opportunities afforded them at the school, but two years at Fairview Junior High School had demonstrated what happened when students were not restrained by adults or each other. The high school was a better place than it had been because more students practiced self-restraint and more adults worked to create an environment in which self-restraint was extolled as a virtue. The school had become a calmer place, at least with regard to fighting.

Even the more optimistic students recognized that much hard work needed to be accomplished before Fairview High School could be considered a good place. They agreed with their principal in this. He, however, saw the quality of his teaching staff as the problem. The students also commented about poor teaching, but they spoke far more about the prevalence of drugs on the street and their continuing presence in the school. Students were well aware of laws that prohibit the selling of drugs anywhere near a school building and require harsh punishments for persons who were caught engaging in such behavior. School administrators had reinforced the seriousness that they attached to drug dealing and drug use by bringing police into the high school in order to search for drugs. The event received a great deal of attention in the local media.

The police search had a sobering effect on the entire student body. Drug dealing on campus would not be tolerated, or so it seemed. The reality of the situation was more complex. Students made a distinction between "hard" drugs such as cocaine and "soft" drugs such as alcohol and marijuana. "Hard" drugs, students told me, ordinarily were not brought on campus after the police raid. "Soft" drugs apparently remained available to anyone who wanted to buy or consume them during the course of a regular school day. An unknown number of students did purchase and ingest them while at school. A good portion of them, however, reportedly came to school having already sampled some alcohol or marijuana or brought these items with them from home.

The police raid notwithstanding, school staff tolerated the presence of "soft" drugs on the campus, and they made no obvious effort to discourage the reintroduction of "hard" drugs to the school. It was the students themselves who were largely responsible for limiting the presence of cocaine on school grounds and being more discreet in their dealing than one might have expected. They made it clear that the exchange of drugs for money on campus was trivial in comparison to what took place away from the school.

One member of A Few Good Men, Germane, tried to put the drug situation at school into perspective. Much of what he told me was later corroborated by students who had more routine contact with drug dealers.

"There's a lot of kids on campus that sell cocaine or crack," Germane said. "Some of the students . . . work together. But as far as I'm like sellin' it to one of my friends to take it? Nah. When it comes to drugs, the funny thing about it is they'll sell it . . . but they won't take it."

"How many will sell while they're on campus?"

"I really can't even say," Germane replied. He noted that it was hard to tell who the drug dealers were since they did not all dress the same. Not all of them wore heavy gold chains and high top sneakers. "Some wear, like, Polo shirts and nice slacks, cologne, and loafers." So, there really was no way to know how many students might be dealing on campus.

"How are deals made on campus?"

"You'll hear somebody say, 'I need some money,' when . . . there's somethin' out there they want."

"They'll sell it on campus?"

"Well, not too much on campus, but that's where the exchanges come from. You know, during lunch hour or before school or after school you might meet your buddy . . . in the parking lot or . . . cafeteria. Go on and get it taken care of because in between class periods there's a lot of people roamin' around and you don't wanta get caught with it."

"Are the dealers from any particular gang?"

"No. It varies. Believe it or not, some of these students doin' it are on the Honor Role for getting high grades. It's not like only the students who don't give a hoot about getting an education."

"Are they gang members?" I asked.

Germane shook his head. "You don't have to be a gang member to sell a few rocks. The whole issue in this deal is money."

"Are the wholesalers gang members?"

He smiled a bit, then said, "You know these guys runnin' around, callin' themselves Crips or Bloods or whatever?"

I nodded my head in agreement.

"Well, that's just a label they've given themselves. It's just you might know somebody . . . that have gone in that type of direction. You don't have to be a member. It's just who you know. They're very picky about the people they trust. The people getting high grades have to keep it to themselves. They need the teachers and students to still think highly of them; but no one really knows what they do after school."

"Most do it to earn spending money?" I asked.

"Yeah. They're doin' it basically to keep a coupla dollars in their pockets. It's not like they're drivin' up to school in nice cars or anything." Or, they do it "to get some money for their prom stuff. Occasionally a dance or something like that comes around. That's when everybody wants to get hold of a few rocks to sell. There'll be a couple who make enough to set it aside . . . and when another event comes along they don't have to worry about it."

"Does selling this stuff bother them?"

"Basically they're nervous the whole time this is going on. They just want to get it as soon as possible and get rid of it so they can make their money."

"If they know the right persons to buy it from, why are they so worried?"

"They've heard of kids who used to go to school here being killed or caught. They're worried about who sees them."

"Does the illegality of their actions bother them?"

"They take that for granted."

"They don't see anything morally wrong in selling it?"

"No, not really. If a person's willing to buy it, they're willing to sell it."

"Is there a lot of alcohol or marijuana on this campus?"

"Probably fewer of them than the number who sell cocaine," Germane replied. "They aren't the same ones who do the cocaine. They sell individual joints for a buck fifty or two dollars. About half of that will be profit."

"How many will buy it on an average day?"

"Probably about twenty people. Some of the same, some different every day. They smoke it here. Know it won't smell by the time they get home."

"How about liquor?"

"I've never really seen much. A lot of them will go home after school and drink."

Other students elaborated upon the ideas expressed by Germane.

I asked two young men from the same town if a lot of students smoked marijuana while on campus.

"It's like this," the first youth said. "They come up to school, man, smellin' like it."

"How many?"

"Maybe five or six."

The second youth laughed. "More than that," he added. "Some bring it to school and sell it to other people. They'll sell a joint for a dollar, dollar fifty."

"But most who smoke or drink do it before school," the first youth interjected. "The smell hits you like a wave. Only about three girls I know up here smoke."

"But the dudes," stated the second teen, "hey, some dudes be bringin' a half pint of gin to school . . . They be comin' here already messed up. They drink it on the bus."

"Surely the teachers must notice this?"

"They send 'em down to the nurse to take their little breathalizer test, man," said the first boy.

"Do they always get sent down?"

"If you're chillin', just sit there and put your head on the desk, they ain't goin' to mess with you. But if you come in ... actin' stupid, they'll probably call security for disruptin' class."

The second youth said, "Sure the teachers know it, but what can they do? Some students called to the office just leave campus."

Other students estimated that between one and two dozen of their peers drank alcohol or smoked marijuana every day, but they emphasized that the same persons did not necessarily do it every day.

One young man said, "You hear people talkin' about drug dealing on campus, but I don't know how many actually do it."

"What about coming to school drunk or stoned?"

"Not that I've noticed. There are times when I've been late to school and had to go to detention. Well, some of the people sittin' there will have this glazed look on their face and all."

"Is it the same persons all the time?"

He shook his head. "Maybe twenty-five come to school this way, but it's not the same ones [all the time]."

Another young man told me, "Yesterday I saw two gentlemen on the second floor drinking a forty ounce bottle of beer."

"Right in the middle of the hallway?"

"Riiight."

"Weren't there any teachers around?"

"Teachers walkin' right past 'em."

"Come on," I said. "You're kidding me, right?"

"Maybe they didn't see 'em, but I saw 'em drinking."

"So drinking and marijuana smoking are done pretty openly?"

"Yup. Everyone knows about it, but they just go about their business."

"Doesn't it interfere with their classes?"

"Well, if you ever visit Mr Smith's class during the third or fourth hour periods, you would see how it affects these people."

"What would I see?"

"A bunch of animals."

"Assuming the man's not dead, he must realize there is a problem," I said.

"He knows."

"What does he do about it?"

"Goes along with the program."

"What does that mean?"

"He teaches through it."

"Doesn't this anger you?"

"Yes."

"Do you report it?"

He shook his head. "No. You just don't understand. It's not just this man's class. It's not just guys. It's not just blacks. It's not just the low achievers who are doin' this."

The purchase and use of drugs at school were noticed, but most students did not engage in such activities. There were, after all, nearly fifteen hundred students enrolled at the high school. If we grant that up to two dozen students were drunk or stoned enough to draw the attention of students or teachers, then between 1 and 2 percent of the student population was impaired to some extent on any given day. School staff were able to continue with their routine chores in the face of at least that much drug use on campus.

"Look," I said a bit strongly to one student, "I smelled it on your breath when you walked in. Your teachers must notice it."

He nodded his head slowly. "Some of 'em'll ask you if you been drinkin', but long as you not actin' crazy, actin' abnormal . . . I may have liquor on my breath, but as far as clownin', actin' up? No. I don't curse out some teacher."

"So teachers don't bring it to you?"

"As long as you're actin' regular . . . You screamin', they may send you down to the office, or send you down to the nurse's office so you can go to sleep."

School staff might pass a bathroom that reeked of marijuana, as I had passed it, and do nothing about it. Or, they might spy a young woman take a quick sip from a bottle hidden in her locker, as I observed one doing, and say nothing to her. The unwritten school policy was to tolerate a small amount of drug use on campus.

A certain amount of drug dealing also was tolerated. I asked one young woman about drug dealing on campus. She said, "I know there is. That's a Y-E-S."

"What is it like?"

"Well last week I was on my way to gym class and there were these three guys behind Ames Hall. I suspect it was some kind of drug activity, because it was really 'hush hush' back there, and they were getting ready to run as I came around the back. They were passing something around. I don't know what it was, but . . ."

"Anything else?"

"I've seen guys with beepers. Mr Turner has made it a rule that no one wears beepers up here, and Mrs Lockwood was chasing this one guy that had a beeper. He denied it was a beeper, but I saw it. There are people up here who still carry beepers, and there are people up here who hold money for drug guys. Girls in particular. There has to be more than a dozen, I'm sure."

"You've seen this?"

"Yes."

"What kind of dollars are we talking about?"

"Fat rolls."

"What do the girls get in return?"

"I think it's money from the guys, because they have stuff that comes from major stores. There are girls who look like they go shopping every single night, but their families got nothin'. They come to school in a new outfit every day . . . I mean like leathurrr . . . from their head to toes, gold chains, gold earrings . . . you name it. And Gucci bags? It's like they got one for every day of the week. They may or may not have come from major department stores. There are places . . . that sell them pretty cheap. I suspect that some of those are hot [stolen], too. From what I understand . . . girls steal things from department stores. My friend works at [a well-known department store], and she said some of them came in regularly."

"To buy or steal?"

"First buy, then steal."

The young women to whom this female was referring were known as "drug whores" or "dope girls," and they really did stick out from the regular student population. They also played an important part in drug dealing on and off campus.

"You can tell who the dope girls are," one knowledgeable teenager told me. " 'Cuz of their earrings . . . big ones like pirates used to wear. Look like you can swing off 'em. Wear all that jewelry. Some just like that style, but most . . . do it 'cause they hang around with dope men or they belong to a dope man. They a dope man's girl."

"What does that mean?"

"Some get it from their man. They try to hold out as long as they can. But when they can't hold out any longer, that's when the sex comes in."

I asked one young woman who knew several "dope girls" how much money might be involved. "It depends on how much the guy makes," she replied. "Let's say he makes five hundred dollars. Maybe a hundred."

"On what will they spend this money?"

"Clothes. Jewelry. You see, I think that's one reason why there's been a rise in drug sellin', because the females like it. Well some do. They like the money and the attention."

She added that girls who received this money told their parents that it had come from their boyfriend as a present. "Didn't the girls or the parents see anything wrong with this?" I asked.

The young women shrugged her shoulders. "Guess not," she said.

"You actually know girls who do this?"

"I know a lot of them," she replied.

"What do the girls say about this arrangement?"

"They brag about it."

"Brag?"

She nodded her head and added, "I know one of my friends . . . she has five or six boyfriends payin' her."

"All at the same time?"

"Yup."

"Are they from the same gang?"

"They're from different groups. Some of them are her relatives; but they're all enemies."

"These guys don't know about this do they?"

"They don't. I'm sure they don't."

"She's playing a dangerous game, isn't she?"

"Yes. And she has a nine-month-old daughter. So she's putting herself and her daughter in danger."

"Does she appreciate the risk?"

"I don't know. She just likes the money. She has almost eight hundred dollars a day at school, at least. And I'm sure she has money at home."

"That's a lot of money," I stated.

"And she doesn't work. And she has a lot of jewelry. All kinds of designer clothes."

"But this is an extreme case, right?"

"You could say that; but there are a lot of girls here that have at least two boyfriends who sell drugs."

"From different gangs?"

"Uhm hum."

"And the boys don't know, right?"

"That's right," she said. "Then there are some that have a regular boyfriend and a boyfriend that sells dope."

"How many girls do this?"

"Maybe about forty. Especially the sophomores have it really bad. But the one who has five or six is a senior. She stays at home with her mother. I really don't think her mother cares."

"In exchange for this money, are there sexual favors offered to the boys?"

"Sometimes," she replied. "Well, most of the time. Let's put it like that."

"Is there a love commitment there?"

"Very seldom. Very seldom. The guys just like to show off. The girls stick around for say two months. Then they move on."

"They circulate from boy to boy?"

"Yes."

"Surely some of the guys must have figured this part out," I stated.

"I'm sure they're aware of it," she answered.

"But it doesn't stop the boys, does it?"

"No it doesn't."

"They just pick up another girl?"

"Uhm hmmm. Most of the time they have more than one girlfriend anyway."

"What do you think about all of this?" I asked.

"I think it's ignorant."

Other students indicated that there were many girls who did this, but not so many as there were boys selling drugs.

"Are there many girls like that?" I asked one young man.

"There's some," he said, "but it's harder to pick out the guys ... who deal, because now guys ... are dressin' better, not like the movie image."

"How many guys sell that you know of?"

"Only five to ten who probably sell it heavily in the community."

"From the same town?"

"No comment."

"Do they sell on campus?"

"No comment."

"How many customers will they have on campus?"

"No more than two or three. You have too many customers, somebody's gonna talk."

"Are any of the customers girls?"

He nodded his head. "If you're a female and have no money but have some gold on, give me all your jewelry and I'll give you this sixteenth."

"You barter?"

"Sometimes. It depends on how hard up he is for cash. If he's not hard up, he'll take the jewelry. Or, if the customer's a guy, he'll take money or his tires ... or his sound system from the car."

"How much is purchased on campus?"

"Not that much. Most of them are really smart; won't carry it in school. They may keep it in their car. You gotta have cause to search their car. They'll make a deal on campus and finish it off campus."

"How much are the transactions on campus worth?"

"Person carries an ounce. That could go in a day. If it's good ... two hundred seventy-five dollars, maybe three hundred."

"Do they do it every day?"

"It may not be for the same amount every day, but more or less everyday. Maybe seventy or eighty dollars' worth."

"About three to four hundred dollars a week for each dope man?"

"That's right."

"So, the six to ten you know making deals on campus pull down three to four thousand a week," I stated.

He did not reply.

Out on the Streets

What happened once students left the safe confines of Fairview High School was less problematic and more sobering. "When you first start out you get real scared," one drug dealer told me.

"Of what or whom?"

"They're scared 'cause they don't know what to do. They don't know how much they're goin' to sell it for. Someone might try to rip them off or something. They're scared."

"How do they learn?"

"From their friends."

"When do they start?"

"Probably junior high school."

"Are they still doing it?"

"They got everything they need. They got everything they want. They got the clothes, jewelry, and all that other stuff."

"Will they stop and not do it again?"

"Nah, it ain't like that. They'll wait a while, wait a while. Then they'll start up again."

Other teens confirmed this story in their interviews.

"How much do you rely on your fellow gang members?" I asked one youth.

"Three people," he replied, "really bring in the big stuff and give it to the other people." In the case of his gang, there were twelve "other people" who did the street-level dealing.

"Do you sell it as a group or independently?"

"Independently. I'll get it from an LA Blood who doesn't live in my neighborhood. You stash your own money, about a thousand dollars, just in case you get caught. Most people want to buy a car and then just get out of the business. Some people talk about doin' it for as long as they live. Most don't. They'll go back into it, if they need the money."

I asked another youth if he ever required the aid of a friend when he dealt drugs.

"I might need some money. You might kick me down some money. I'd pay you back. You know. I might need an ounce right then and there, if I've got a big deal comin' down. Ya know. 'I'll meet you somewhere at six o'clock and we'll make the swap,' I'd say. 'You watch my back, while I make this hit right quick.' You know. Somethin' like that. They're real tight. They hangin' together."

"If I help you like that, will you give me something?"

"Absolutely. You know, we're like . . . brothers. After all, that's money you lost . . . product you didn't have to sell. I'll pay you back. 'Cuz when you're in dope you have no friends. You have no boys. You have no friends, because your boys are the same ones you're competing against. You never know what's goin' on in their heads. They may want to move up on you a little bit. It's business."

I found it more than a little interesting that he could speak of a fellow drug dealer as a brother and, at the same time, all but dismiss the possibility that one of these brothers also could be a friend. It was important only that he had no difficulty keeping this distinction safely tucked away in his brain and called upon it in order to make sense of his relations with some of his peers.

"What if you don't pay back your loans?" I asked.

"Then somethin's goin' to happen to ya."

"Are you afraid?"

"If ya gotta go, you gotta go," he replied. "But," he added as an afterthought, "it depends on how you go."

The cops hassle them, take their money, or beat them up. Rarely do the cops arrest them. That, too, is part of the price of doing business. When business is good, even the littlest street dealer can make as much as five hundred dollars in a week. That certainly is a great deal of money, but it comes at a price. Whatever social support might be provided in a fictive family is sacrificed to a grim brotherhood based on nothing more substantial than money garnered from the sale of an addictive white powder.

One young woman told me that about half the boys in her town's gang sold drugs and half worked at regular jobs. Some of the dealers "save their money so they can get out of it," she said. "Others just spend it on stuff and their girlfriends."

"What do those who want to get out of it say about their activity?"

"They know it's dangerous. They say it's the only way they can make it. So, they're goin' to do it 'til they can get on their feet."

"How much does that take?"

"Fifty thousand dollars."

"Is that the number they use?"

"Yes. Or, a hundred thousand. They'll spend about half of what they make. Not many are saving to get out. Maybe three or four. Others are saving so they can get their own stuff and be as big as the guy they're sellin' for."

"Do they sell it as a group?"

"Sometimes . . . but rarely."

"Sell it in or outside of the neighborhood?"

"Both."

Another teen said that the eighteen members of his group did sell drugs cooperatively. "How does it work?" I asked.

"Like three at a time will work a spot," he answered.

"Do they get their stuff from the same Crip all the time?"

"Yes."

"Do they split their profits equally?"

"Yes. Each is making about a thousand dollars a week. They only started two months ago."

Oakdale and Riveredge had two of the larger drug dealing gangs. "They call 'em 'Crime-edge' and 'Drugdale,' " a teenager told me. His street name was "Ropes" because he had liked to wear heavy gold chains when he went out in public. He was a big boy who was not shy about his accomplishments.

"If they're big, Ropes, how big are they?"

"Ninety percent of all the fancy cars come from Oakdale and Riveredge," he said. "With the fancy wheels, systems, rag top . . . more than fifteen grand."

"Okay Ropes. How many from Oakdale deal? Don't be modest."

Ropes laughed. "It's between none and a third. Ten to fifteen."

"How many do it every day?"

"Virtually none. They'll wait 'til the start of the month when welfare checks come in. Or, they'll do it on the weekends." He paused and scratched his chin. "Let's see. Today's the third. Ought to be big checks out there." He chuckled.

"On those days you're selling, how much is each of you going to make?"

"From the first to the fifth, five grand."

"How much of that is profit?"

"Half. Something like that. Won't make much more on weekends. Welfare days are *The big ones*," he said with great emphasis.

"Does it bother them to sell to such people?"

"No," he said without hesitation. "They got money. Got their cars."

"Do they plan to sell for a long time?"

"No. They do it to get some money real quick. One week they might be into it. Next week not. Might last awhile. Then end it. Start up a month or two later."

"What about the summer?"

"During the summer? Open season, 'cause you're doin' nothin' all day long."

"Lots of competition?"

"That's what I don't understand. How people are making so much money with so many people sellin' drugs. You got to go somewhere that has the action."

"Where might that be?"

"The city. Got your poverty-stricken families and all. That welfare comes in . . ."

"Don't you have trouble with the city gangs because you're moving in on their territories?"

"That's why people make friends there."

"Don't the local cops know what you're doing?"

Ropes nodded his head in agreement. "Most of the cops are paid off," he said, than paused. "Well, I couldn't say 'most.' I'll say some do. The cops around here sell dope, too."

"From where do they get it?"

"Off the kids. They, like, stop kids. They take they money, dope, and stuff. But instead of turnin' it in, some of 'em keep it. They like beat the kids."

"I've heard that Officer Jones from your town takes kickbacks."

"Uh . . . I wouldn't care to say."

"Doesn't it bother you?"

"Some kids accept it. Some try to get back at the cop."

"How?"

"They might shoot at the police car."

"Is that the cop's price for doing business?"

Ropes nodded his head, once. I changed the subject.

"Do a lot of the kids at this school sell drugs?"

"Some that I know of. Not too many . . . for one thing it's kind of hard to find some now. It's not goin' out like it was last year. It's harder to find guys cookin' it up and puttin' it out as rock. That knocked out a lot of the smaller guys." Ropes chuckled. "A lot of 'em went to work. Work in a fast food place."

"Competition too stiff?"

Ropes shook his head, "Can't get the product from the middle man. A lot of the bigger guys gettin' locked up."

"Does that seem to scare them? Or would they still sell, if they could get the stuff?"

"A lot would do it, if they could find it. A lot of times, if it do come in, they'll get it and sell it. After you already tried it, tried sellin' yourself, that's money comin' in. It's like a habit, like a user. It's comin' so good, you know, why stop it? You know what I'm sayin'. It's like a habit. You feel you gotta do it. The money's comin' easy. You wanna buy this. You wanna buy a car. Some of 'em when they get it . . . they won't touch the dope no more. They get high enough, they just have other people doin' for 'em. Lots just stop. Leave it alone. Get a job. Some of 'em do it like that. On a spree."

"My impression," I stated, "is that only a few kids from each gang are selling routinely."

"That's it," Ropes said. "Maybe half do it at all, if you count those doin' it on a spree. If they get product to sell, they'll hold it . . . to the first of the month when everybody gets checks, and everybody goin' to cash they check. They'll wait 'til that certain time, and in two days they can sell it. There's a lot of money circulatin', so . . . you can make a killin' and then wait 'til next month."

"What's a killing?"

"Maybe forty-two hundred in two days."

"Aren't they worried about doing this?"

"A lot of them already caught a case. So they tryin' to cool out some.

The next time they get caught, you may not be so lucky. You may not get probation. You may have to do the time. A lot of them get scared, 'cause a lot of them got locked up. But they'll keep doin' it 'til they get caught."

"Why do they sell it?"

"Well some of them do it 'cause their parents do it. Some do it 'cause that's what some girls like. They want to get considered a 'dope man' so they can get a dope girl ... but they're not for-real girls. Some guys start to realize that and let 'em go. A lot of 'em spend so much on [dope girls]. They stop dealin' with drugs then. There's a lot of things that make 'em do it. And there's a lot of things that make 'em stop doin' it.'"

"Fear of being shot?"

"Naaah."

"That doesn't bother them?"

"Some guys. But me personally myself, it didn't bother me ... I went out in these neighborhoods. When the Bloods came in, they started givin' everybody ounces. They say, 'You wanna work? We give you an ounce.' Maybe two ounces, three ounces. They gave it to you. But I wasn't goin' to work for none of that, 'cause I believe once you're in it, it's hard to get out of it. So I worked for myself, me and my cousin. I was in it just to make some money and put some into an account. I normally was out there every day, though. Givin' money to the girlfriend. Gettin' up clothes for the baby and all. So that's why I was mostly doin' it. I'm on probation now for doin' it, and I thought next time I might not be so lucky. I wouldn't get probation. I'd get a one-way ticket to the state penitentiary."

"Is that why people drop out of it?"

"Lot of their peers startin' to think differently about the matter. Sellin' drugs is not, you know, like it used to be. Why take the risk? To get locked up? Maybe shot and killed? Messin' with blood money ... Some guys, they parents tell them to leave it alone. It's a lot of different things that make 'em stop. The one's that are gettin' in it ... they don't know yet. Unless somebody talk to 'em and tell 'em to stop hangin' with the groups that's influencin' them to do that kind of thing ..."

"They're in for trouble?"

Ropes nodded his head, once.

Another teen still in the trade held a different view. His gang was far better organized than the little one with which Ropes had been affiliated, and it showed in how he described its operation. His name was Nicky.

"How many of you do it routinely?" I asked.

"In our neighborhood," he replied, "it mainly be teenagers, maybe two or three adults. They'll pull in fifty grand a week."

"How much of that is profit?"

"I'll say about thirty-five." He really was not certain.

"How about the kids? How much can they make?"

On a good week, he said, each of several dozen youngsters who sold drugs might make five hundred dollars. They spent the money on cars, clothes, and jewelry.

"Some money in your gang was set aside in a bail fund, wasn't it?"

Nicky looked a little surprised, but he answered the question. "Yes."

"Did everyone kick into it?"

"Yes. Maybe 5 percent of your pay."

"Anything else purchased with that 5 percent?"

"Some will go to guns and other stuff for the whole group."

"Any go to real estate?"

Again Nicky looked surprised. "They may buy a store or somethin'."

"A lot of property?"

"Just one building."

"What is it used for?"

"They opened a shop, like a clothing store."

"They rent space to a legitimate business?"

"Right."

"The rental payments are put back into the common fund?"

"Yeah, but some goes to the big guys who buy our stuff."

"Any other spinoff businesses at this time?"

"No."

"Are there times when profits go to someone in the hood who needs help?"

Nicky was puzzled. His expression conveyed the idea that I either knew a great deal about his gang or was really good at guessing what questions to ask.

"Yes," he said in a reserved way. "This may happen often. Kids may need to come to school, but they stay in the hood. They need clothes. We lay out two, three hundred dollars for some clothes."

"Those whom you are helping need not be active in the gang, right?"

"Right." The assistance was offered to persons who were "down with the neighborhood."

"How often does that happen?" I asked.

"Mostly, I'll say, once a month or so. It's not a routine thing."

"Do anything special with the little kids?"

Nicky didn't say anything at first, but looked at me in a way that showed that he no longer wondered if I were a lucky guesser. "Built 'em a little playground in the neighborhood with some profits."

"What are we talking about?"

"Swings. Slides. In a little park. I think it cost five grand."

"Anything else that you've done?"

"No. That's about it." He looked at me as if to say, "But you knew that already, didn't you?"

Young men and women with whom I spoke about the prospect of earning money through illegal means were of two minds. Many were not bothered by the prospect of earning money in this way. Others did not like it or were frightened away from it. As one young man told me, "I got a job. Makin' some good money."

"What are you doing?"

"Bussin' tables at a restaurant. I also make salads in the kitchen."

"You say that you earn 'pretty good money.' How much would that be?"

"I'm makin' five dollars and fifty cents an hour. Goin' to get a raise in two weeks." He was proud of that.

"On an average week, how much will you pull in?"

"My highest check ... was four hundred and fifty dollars for a week." Usually, he earned about two hundred dollars. He spent a portion of it, but also put some of it away. This, he said, enabled him to stay out of the drug trade.

It was steadier work than selling drugs, and he probably did not make much less money than the average street dealer. There was no doubt that he had to work longer hours to get his money. On the other hand, cops did not hassle him and he did not worry about being cheated by a friend or shot by a customer.

Another young man was more sympathetic to the desire of his peers to have fancy items from stores and to be known for being part of a dangerous trade. Yet he also appreciated how marginal these accomplishments really were. His words were expressed with great passion.

"Some people sell drugs because that's what they have to do," or so they think. "You don't have to do it," he said. "You have an alternate, [but] most do it because they wanta get somethin'. They want somethin' nice. But that's life, especially if you're black. I mean to us it's like ... we wanta get somethin'. But what [blacks] fail to realize is they still don't have nothin'. People who are mean to us, Caucasians who are mean to us who have big businesses, to them we're small time. You ain't nothin'. You gotta coupla thousand in yah pocket, you got a lot of money, right? To them ... it's nothin'. But to us it's some nice clothes, put a nice system in your car ... stuff our people can't afford. To white people it's piss."

This young man was telling me something important, and it had little to do with my putative race or wealth. After all, as he himself noted, we all want something nice, or at least better, for ourselves. It simply, and unfortunately, was harder for some of us to attain that end. The power and great truth in his words came from the realization that his peers had secured only the illusion of progress and purchasing parity with whites by engaging in a fast and dangerous enterprise. They "still don't have nothin'," he said.

Indeed, compared to the other teen who worked in a restaurant, they may have come out of their experience with less than nothing. The busboy and salad maker had been introduced to the conventional economy and was creating a work history for himself that could be presented to subsequent employers. Street dealers accomplished nothing comparable to this.

I strongly suspect that there were not enough entry-level jobs available in the local economy to have satisfied all potential applicants from the Fairview School District. I know that younger children certainly would not have found jobs in the regular economy that paid hundreds of dollars. On the other hand, no child has any need or right to have discretionary power over such large amounts of money.

Many children and adolescents were introduced to organized and remunerated work through criminal enterprises. The habits formed as a result of those experiences were not ones that most of us would think in their best interest or our own. One can take small but real comfort, however, from the knowledge that many young persons apparently had figured that out for themselves. Most moved into the trade when they needed money, left the trade when their needs were met, and expected or hoped to find gainful employment in the regular economy at some point in the future.

There were other important signs that older adolescents appreciated the seriousness of their situation and tried to restrain themselves. Foremost among these signs was the reluctance of local gang members to increase the level of violence in their fights with opposing townships. Many had access to guns, but they were more likely to wave the weapon in the air than to shoot it and to shoot away from people rather than at them. Older adolescents apparently continued the behavior they had witnessed first as young teenagers. They were more interested in scaring an opponent than in injuring him.

The introduction of deadly force into gang fights came largely by way of drug dealing and the presence of non-local gangs such as the Bloods and Crips. Gang members from different towns, tied as they sometimes were by friendship and family relations, said that they tried to separate deadly force from drug dealing inside their neighborhoods. They did not always succeed. Nevertheless, the number and severity of gunshot injuries, as reported by the media and the teens themselves, were far less in these towns than in the city located just a few miles away. Even more important, perhaps, members of several local gangs affiliated with different Los Angeles gangs spoke of their separate efforts to constrain resident Crips and Bloods, even to the point of forcing the LA drug dealers out of their neighborhoods.

There is no way of knowing whether or how long the municipal gangs could resist being drawn into the spiral of violence overtaking other places.

For the time being, though, they were succeeding. Their loyalty to the neighborhoods in which they lived evoked a more conservative tradition in gang behavior that made gangs the protectors of their home turf and those who lived there. Violence in the form of communal brawls is an integral part of that tradition. Murder is not.

Drug dealing and the murderous violence it spawns are a visible repudiation of that tradition insofar as local people are hurt by these activities. Local gang members do sell drugs to individuals in their municipality and sometimes harass them. They often express disdain for their fellow townsmen and violate existing standards for appropriate public behavior.

How local gang members eventually will reconcile these seemingly irreconcilable ways of making gangs and behaving like gang members cannot be known. It was clear when I met with the teenagers who would be responsible for fashioning a lasting response to this dilemma, however, that they were working on a solution.

One young man fretted over the increased availability of guns, and he knew they were being used in fights between local gangs. "How many persons are shot?" I inquired.

"Most of 'em just shoot up."

"You mean up in the air?"

"Over their heads or to the side of 'em. To make a point."

"Why?"

"Most of 'em scared they'll go to jail or get caught."

"So, most of the time they try to miss?"

"Right."

"And if someone is hit, it's an accident?"

"Most of the time."

"How did this come to be?"

"It just worked out that way. In the light, people aim away during big gang fights because they don't want to be followed by the guys they shot at." He went on to explain that people would use guns in drive-by shootings and sometimes during a fight against someone with whom they had a private disagreement. No one wanted to see conditions like those in the city where "everybody shoots *at you* any time of the day." Most teenagers with whom I spoke had never seen anyone shot in these fights. Those who had, or knew someone who was shot, spoke soberly about the experience.

Neighborhoods and Families

It may seem foolish to say that students were more restrained in the high school, given the ready availability of some types of drugs and the continuing fights between individuals from different towns. Yet more than wishful thinking informs my assessment of their behavior. Drugs and guns were no less available to them than they were to young persons in any city, but they were not sold or used with such open contempt as is the case in many urban school districts. It may have been, as a number of students said, that they did a lot more in the city than in their barely suburban municipalities. They certainly were familiar with many of the city gangs and conversant with the gangs' territories, activities, and members. Their knowledge of the city's landscape and personal testimony aside, it was nonetheless true that their high school was a great deal calmer and less obviously corrupted by ongoing gang activity than many inner-city high schools. The reasons for this were to be found in the tone set for the school by its principal and students.

No matter what school officials had tried to do, however, none of it would have succeeded even marginally without the cooperation of the students. The comparative peace and quiet of Fairview High School was real, but it was accomplished less by design than by the application of hard lessons students learned on the streets and in the junior high school. No matter how much the young people from one town may have disliked those from another town, they were stuck with each other. They were settled in towns with fixed borders and a common school district. There was no place to run. The situation they faced was not very different from that which had confronted the United States and the former Soviet Union. These two great nations, political scientist Edwin Fedder was fond of saying, were delivered from the worst excesses of their own behavior by the inescapable reality that they were condemned to a dialogue. It was no different for gang members in these towns. They had to find a way to coexist.

The dialogue in which gang members from the Fairview School District engaged began in their families and neighborhoods. I have no way of knowing how many parents of high school students knew their sons or daughters were engaged in serious delinquent behavior. Judging by what the youngsters said, however, no small portion of the parents must have had strong suspicions and did not complain too loudly or long. Too many of the students with whom I spoke referred to their own or their fellow gang members' parents quietly accepting the money offered to them by a child with no apparent job. Other parents were said to have openly confronted their children about dealing drugs and were told about their child's involvement.

Students told me that parents nearly always asked their children to be careful. Beyond that the reaction varied. Some parents were said to have made an effort to stop their child from selling drugs. When that failed, they either asked the child to leave the home or acquiesced and accepted some of the child's earnings. A small number of students stated that parents introduced their children to the drug trade, and there appeared to be more than a little evidence in school files to back up that perception. These parents took a good portion of the money acquired by a son in this way. It seemed that everyone was aware of the risks attendant to being a drug dealer, and most parents made at least some effort to restrain or curb their child's involvement in the trade.

There was other pressure for youngsters to remain in the drug trade, and much of it centered on the youth's desire or the parents' need for money. One young man estimated that at least half of the youthful drug dealers he knew gave their parents several hundred dollars each week. They often did this, he said, after their parents noticed changes in their style of dress.

"Do parents ask for money once this happens?" I asked.

"No," he replied, "the kid just gives it to them. I guess, you know, some people want to play the role like they be workin' and givin' their parents the check."

"But the parents know better, don't they?"

"Right. They know better."

"They going to say anything to the kid?"

"No. They'll just say, 'If you're goin' to do it, don't bring it to my house, and watch your back.' "

"Do parents enjoy the extra money?"

"No. Some parents don't. It's just that the way it is now, parents can't do nothin' but accept the wage. Hard times what they is, you know. Some people may be laid off . . . that's why they accept the money."

"Are you saying that it is an important source of income for the family?"

"Yeah."

"Do they *really* need that money?"

"Well, my mother or father do not need no money like that. They got a job. But some people's mother enjoy it."

"Do your parents know?"

"My mother doesn't. My father brought it to me. He said to watch my back. It ain't nothin' to play with."

Another youth said he knew of seven boys who gave their parents money. "This one guy I know," he continued, "I asked him if his mother knew."

"And did she?"

"Yes. She said she didn't care, 'cause she used to do it when she was little."

"What do kids think of their parents when they buy the parents off that way?"

"Then they don't have to hide it anymore. They move out, get their own apartment. Some parents try to get to the bottom of it. Other parents are into it just as much as the kid. Probably got their kids into it."

"When you say that they move out, you must be talking about the bigger dealers," I stated. "The smaller dealers still live at home, right?"

"Most do."

"Do their parents know about it?"

"No, for the simple fact that a lot of people I know that sell . . . don't own big, rich, fancy cars. They wear gold and nice clothes, and they got a job. But they'll catch a bus to school. It's like a cover for 'em. Far as the parents . . . the kids won't do nothin' out of the ordinary to give 'em suspicion. Because a lot of people, believe it or not, respect their parents . . . they won't [bring] it in their house or nothing like that."

"But some parents know," I stated.

"Yes."

"What do these parents do?"

"Ain't too much they can do. I mean you can't put the kid out . . ."

"Maybe not, but some parents charge their child rent, right?"

"Yeah, I've known that to happen."

"Four, five, six hundred dollars a month?"

"That's about on the nose. But you have to understand, a lot of parents aren't well off. The kid puts a little money in his own pocket so he don't have to ask his parents for none."

Another knowledgeable young man indicated that parents "don't want to think about their kid involved with dope."

"And what about those parents who think that they have to say something to their kid?" I asked.

"Well, the first couple of times they'll try to get 'im to stop. Then pretty soon they let it be. 'Cuz they figure like, 'He's bringin' in money, so that's more money for the household.' And that way they don't have to take care of him no more. Pretty soon [they're] gonna start askin' for money."

"How much?"

"Hundreds."

"How many kids do you know like that?"

"Five to ten. And some parents sell with their kids. Most of the time the parents bring the kid into it. The kids learn by watchin' their parents."

One young woman added a point that no male had mentioned. She said that "some parents can't say anything to their kids because they're too scared of 'em."

I knew this to have happened in some instances, but I doubted that it covered the majority of cases. I simply observed that many teenagers had a rather contemptuous attitude toward adults.

She nodded her head in agreement. "I guess they just didn't have any good role models. Their parents haven't been there for them. When you don't have a good parent . . . You're gonna feel like this person is not worth your time even though it's your parent."

"Does the same thing hold for teachers?"

"Yes. And it's especially there for black kids who say, 'No white person can tell me anything.'"

How much of this attitude toward white teachers was based on prejudice is hard to say. Some part of it undoubtedly was. Yet I had heard older boys and girls make equally contemptuous remarks about parents and especially about the grown-ups to whom they sold drugs. Many of the teenagers with whom I spoke were not particularly keen on grown-ups or the prospect of becoming one themselves. Granted, this does not distinguish boys and girls in gangs from most other teens. What does distinguish them and their attitude toward adults, however, is the cynicism and passion with which these views are expressed.

After I had talked to a few hundred teenagers it became clear to me that they made a distinction in their own minds between competent and incompetent adults. They did not like competent adults, who set limits, held them to high standards, and generally were a nuisance. But although teenagers were not fond of such people they did respect their behaving this way. Incompetent grown-ups – parents in the drug trade, teachers who didn't teach, crack heads, and crooked cops – were not worthy of respect. Indeed, in the minds of many teenagers, these people were scum who deserved whatever awful fate befell them.

We all have known competent and incompetent adults. The problem for many of the youngsters with whom I spoke was that they had known more incompetent grown-ups. They held many adults in low regard because so few had given them much reason to be respectful. This was part of the reason why young persons were willing to turn more to each other for support and guidance than to the adults they met every day. Many teens found ways to measure their adulthood on the street, a set of standards they could meet, and readily available ways of being tested to see if they were competent and worthy of respect. More often than not they succeeded.

"When Oakdale tests new members," a young man named Omar told me, "they really beat 'em up. It's like party animals. They get drunk. When we do it in Banister, it's just like boxin'. Hit each other in the chest. It's not a serious thing."

"But has your group been tested in Oakdale?" I inquired.

Omar grinned. "Yeah, we've been tested in their neighborhood . . . a couple of times we went over there."

He seemed proud of this. I asked him why his gang had courted a fight with a much larger gang.

Omar replied, "They want to see how good we are. They hear things about Banister. I tell my friends over there, 'Don't come here and startin' trouble . . . 'cause if we have to fight, then we'll do that."

"Is testing supposed to determine which neighborhood is tougher? Or, is it a way of showing and earning respect?" I asked.

"It's basically . . . respect . . . to see if you're up for your neighborhood. After we fought, then everybody shakes hands and everything. It ain't no

Crip or Blood thing." This meant that neither gang was out to kill their opponents.

Omar noted that his gang respected the Crips and Bloods. "They can deal drugs all they want. We just don't want them in our neighborhood. There are a lot of wannabes walkin' round with their pants hangin' low sayin', 'What's up Cuz.' I hope they don't come down and force the kids in our neighborhood to sell their drugs. The Bloods just came in to see what was happening, and I talked with them. They asked what the children were out there doin'. I said, 'Nah, it's like mostly everybody's workin' in my neighborhood.' They said, 'I can understand that. It's hard since we're deep in it. It's kinda hard for us to get a job [while selling] the white girl they call cocaine.' They understand what we're tryin' to do."

Other young men from different towns corroborated the story that representatives of the Crips and Bloods were leaving them alone. They noted, however, that this was not necessarily because the LA gang-bangers respected the locals' interest in holding jobs in the conventional economy.

"Crips are fightin' Bloods," one teenager told me. "We just don't want it in our territory. We'll still buy from 'em. Just don't want their shit goin' down here."

"Your guys fought the Crips?"

"Yes."

"And they moved out?"

"Yes."

Another teen named Tony said that both Bloods and Crips had tried to move into his town. "Tryin' to take over. Tryin' to lay down the law. But before they did that . . . we got them."

"What do you mean by that?"

"We, you know, moved them out. Discouraged them."

"How severely did you discourage them?"

"Even as far as shootin' at 'em," Tony replied.

"Anybody hurt?"

"Nah. But shots were fired."

"How long did this go on?"

"Started at the end of last summer and is continuing on now . . . but only at the skating rink."

"How many of the guys from your town identify with Crips or Bloods?"

"About fifty of each."

"And they understood what you were trying to do?"

Tony smiled a small, but knowing smile. "No choice but to understand it," he said.

"How long did it take the outsiders to leave town?"

"It didn't take them no time."

"Have they tried to move back in?"

"Noooo."

"It's interesting," I observed, "that the kids from your town who identify with different LA gangs were able to look beyond their colors."

The young man looked at me soberly. "The heavy drug dealing is a danger to everybody," he noted. "Everybody respects their neighborhood. You know? We do stupid things. We fight. They shoot. But if that Crip and Blood stuff comes, there'll be a lot more of it."

"So all you guys from the same town reached something of an understanding, even though you're tied to different LA gangs?"

"Yes."

"Why?"

"You see, most of us grew up with each other. So we're kinda reluctant . . ."

"To get into it?"

"Yeah. For the reason that at one time or another we've been in each other's homes and spent time with the other person."

"So they understand that one part of town went one color, while the other side went a different color?"

"Yeah," Tony replied, "although I find no logic in it."

I could understand his confusion and excuse his inability to make sense of the complex relation among families, neighborhoods, and gangs that had emerged during the lifetime of the children and teenagers who spoke with me. On one level it really did not make much sense. The two most feared and hated confederations of gangs in the United States had established a presence in the same town, and local gang members had aligned themselves with one or the other. However, at the same time these very gang members were carrying out their role as local sales representatives in the wholesale distribution system laid out by the Bloods and Crips, they also were pushing the Californians out of their town. There were no hard feelings. It was only business.

Local gangbangers felt a sense of pride and responsibility for their town, even as they sold poison to some of its inhabitants. They hoped to avoid the nastier and more deadly aspects of the drug trade for their community, even as they profited from it. They divided themselves into warring camps and tried not to go to war. It may have been only business, but it was a confusing business. The great surprise was not that this arrangement was confusing, however, but that young people were able to make it work for themselves and seemed comfortable with it.

They were not alone. The adults in their lives seemed comfortable with this arrangement as well. At least they did not seem particularly keen to do much of anything about their children's involvement with gangs. There were no community meetings at which outraged parents spoke about losing their children to gangs and drug dealing; the police seemed satisfied to make occasional arrests; and many school staff who were in a position to know about such things appeared indifferent. They, too, were going along with the program.

Note

1 James Q. Wilson and Richard J. Herrnstein, *Crime and Human Nature* (New York: Simon & Schuster, 1985); Curt R. Bartol and Anne M. Bartol, *Juvenile Delinquency: a Systems Approach* (Englewood Cliffs, NJ: Prentice Hall, 1989); Daniel J. Monti, Origins and Problems of Gang Research in the United States," in Scott Cummings and Daniel J. Monti (eds) *Gangs: the Origins and Impact of Contemporary Youth Gangs in the United States* (Albany, NY: State University of New York Press, 1993): pp. 3–26.

5

Learning to Ride a Bicycle

This much I can say with certainty. Children are not supposed to act this way. Their lives ought not to be shaped by the customary rhythms of drug deals and brawls. They should not have to swagger down school corridors or neighborhood streets in order to feel in control of their lives or merely good about themselves. It is wrong that they intimidate persons and disrupt their own communities. It is an outrage that they fight and kill each other with dangerous weapons. Whatever childhood and adolescence are supposed to be, this surely is not it.

Few of us probably have seen gangs or had any direct contact with them. Nevertheless, the exploits of gang members have been burned into our brains through a barrage of newspaper stories, magazine articles, mediocre movies, and even worse television talk shows on the subject. They have inspired politicians to make speeches and pass laws, pushed police to make arrests and shakedowns, and prompted would-be reformers to do good or at least to study the bad things gangs do. The rest of us are simply scared.

We really have not figured out what to do about gangs and the harm they cause. For the time being, at least, we seem content to make a lot of principled noise about gangs and not look too foolish. This may make us feel better, but it is unlikely to make any difference to gang members or to have much impact on what they do. Gang members have thought for some time that we adults are pretty foolish, and they are not terribly disturbed by occasional attempts to cure them of their wicked ways.

Sometimes, however, even the toughest of gang members can be surprised by the rare flash of insight or sanity expressed by an adult. Who knows? Maybe this will be one of those moments.

I am a scientist of sorts, one of those people who often find themselves studying bad or discomforting things and who are sometimes called upon to render sage advice on troubling matters. Gangs certainly rank high on our "discomfort scale" and probably would qualify as something that most of us see as being bad. As it happens, I have read a number of books and academic papers that deal with gangs and have done a fair amount of research on the subject myself. At this moment, in fact, I am surrounded by several stacks of documents and books, written mostly by others, that purport to tell me how to make sense of gangs and what we can do to control them. Armed with all that information, I wish that I could say, "This is what it all means, and here's how you fix it."

Unfortunately, I cannot say this, at least not without swallowing really hard or choking on my words. Researchers like myself are still trying to put together a broad outline of all that gangs do and mean to their members. We have not begun to worry about filling in the details of that outline. Much of what is significant about the violence, drugs, and despair that are part of contemporary gangbanging still eludes us, and it seems that we can do little more than offer poor guesses as to how gangs can be made less threatening.

In another age, I suppose, one would have turned to ministers or priests, politicians, and business leaders for solutions to problems caused by gangs. We would have heeded their advice and felt better for it, even if it did not make the world much safer or prettier. What you would not have known, in all likelihood, was that these important persons probably would have turned to someone like me for whatever answers they threw out to a troubled public. Not a comforting thought.

Today, people like me have been pretty successful at cutting out the middleman. We do a little research on our own, often with modest amounts of assistance from a private foundation or government agency, or we read other persons' research and we head straight for you, the troubled public. We do not wait for commissions to be appointed or ministers to come unglued. After all, it was not until November 1993 that Jesse Jackson finally said out loud what many persons had been thinking for a long time. Too many black adolescents were killing or impregnating each other and selling drugs. I will say this much for him. Once he acknowledged that these were serious problems, Jackson was not bashful about trying to involve everybody in his newest crusade. "I am rather convinced," he told one reporter, "that the premier civil rights issue of this day is youth violence."[1]

One might take issue with his characterization of youth violence and drug dealing as civil rights issues or simply be shocked that it took so long for him to figure out that these problems required our immediate attention. His statement may be noteworthy because he is a prominent public figure, but he is hardly the only person in a position of responsibility to have ignored gangs, drugs, and youth violence for too long. Several years ago, for instance, a regional director of the United States Commission on Civil Rights did his utmost to impede the members of one state advisory committee from exploring gang activities as a civil rights issue and, when he could not stop the work from going forward, saw to it that the offending members of the committee were not reappointed. Since then, gang violence and drug dealing have exploded in two of the states for which he was responsible. I take some encouragement, therefore, from the words of Jesse Jackson and other minority leaders no matter how late they have been in coming. Perhaps we finally are ready to see youth violence and drug dealing as challenges to the rights and responsibilities that come with one's membership in this society.

Today, some forty years after the historic *Brown* decision was handed down by the United States Supreme Court, we continue to hear harsh words about our society's alleged racist ways and the damage such ingrained practices cause. Racial discrimination and prejudice certainly remain with us, but they are not reinforced with the power of law or an ideology based on fear and hate. Nor are they the sources of the behavior that I have described in this book. Young people belonged to gangs long before we talked about civil rights and wrongs involving minority citizens. Furthermore, when youngsters wage war on each other and are willing to poison a substantial portion of the population who are left watching the carnage, something more than their civil rights is at risk.

This might be viewed as an admission that we failed to fulfill the moral and practical obligations implied in the *Brown* decision and other pieces of legislation. Or, it may simply be that we now see the futility of making grand and open-ended gestures. I prefer, instead, to view these problems as part of a larger legacy of building or failing to build communities that work. Our progress in dealing with the challenges posed by youth violence and drug dealing will be better measured by the communities minority citizens build for themselves. It will not be secured by the demands of minority leaders that we find a way to climb out of the racist hole we once occupied or the empty rhetoric of politicians who will ask us for more or bigger shovels.

Jesse Jackson was correct in pointing out that we all have a stake in what many young people are doing to themselves and their neighborhoods. I think Minister Don Muhammad, religious leader of Boston's Mosque No. 11, came closer to the thinking of many concerned persons outside of those neighborhoods when he said of Jackson's conversion, "We certainly would accept assistance from anyone who would help. But, this whole thing is like learning to ride a bicycle. At some point you have to take the training wheels off and do it for yourself."[2] A few months later at a conference in Washington, DC, Jesse Jackson, Bill Cosby, and other prominent black citizens repeated the idea that solutions to many of these problems would have to emerge from the minority community itself. It was a promising moment.

As to pushy social scientists who earn their keep by pointing out why training wheels may or may not be needed and how well or poorly they work, much more will be said in this chapter. I will begin by noting that we stopped waiting for permission to bring unpleasant pieces of information to the public some time ago, and we hardly ever get to ride the shiniest bike in the store. This makes us cranky as we go about the tiresome work of writing articles and books that no one seems to read or take seriously. We scurry about for interviews, and we try to draw as much attention to our work, and to ourselves, as we can in order to make a tiny dent in the armor that shields us from the reality of what our children are doing to each other and what we adults are failing to do about it.

Most researchers are fairly responsible and sometimes present a good picture of how gangs are organized and gang members behave under different circumstances. That may not seem like much of an accomplishment, but it is an important first step in figuring out what might be done to curb the awful slaughter and poisoning taking place in too many of our communities today. A prudent person, however, would not wait for social scientists to come up with a definitive answer to his or her questions about gangs. Neither I nor any academic wizard is likely to discover a cure for the common gangbanger.

What I can do is provide some insight into how gangs in the suburbs and schools that I know compare to gangs that others have described in inner-city neighborhoods and schools. I also can draw attention to the approaches that would-be reformers have used in the past to constrain gangs or to turn youngsters away from gangs. I am not at all certain that my observations will prove reassuring or that my words will sound particularly confident. On the other hand, I know that without such a discussion none of us will be able to do anything to make gangs less threatening, and we are more likely to make matters a great deal worse than they already are.

My purpose will not be to convince you that gangs are something other than you imagine or know them to be, but rather to show you that they are not only the stuff of which nightmares are made. I will try to show how the world of gangs can be drawn closer to the world that we occupy and need to make more available to their members. This will be a pretty speculative venture, and many persons may be inclined to dismiss it out of hand. To do so would be a mistake, I think. Researchers like myself may seem at times to have run out of novel ways of thinking about gangs and the young persons who populate them. This does not mean, however, that on occasion we will not discover something that can help us make a little better sense of gangs. I believe that studying and writing about gangs that pop up in the last places you would expect to find them, places like suburbs and schools, will enable us to make better sense of gangs everywhere else.

I hope that those who read this book will take its message seriously. It is far more likely, however, that they will expect gangs somehow to miss their towns or simply go away. Until recently, such thinking might have been dismissed as foolishness; but that is no longer the case. A shaky truce called by leaders of opposing gangs in Los Angeles following the 1992 rioting in that city has given these optimists reason to believe that the worst excesses of gang behavior are now behind us. They note that the truce is holding and may spread to other parts of the United States.

If the truce does spread, then no small part of the credit will be taken by more than one hundred gang members from across the country who met first in late April and early May of 1993 in Kansas City and later again that same year in Chicago. They discussed how such a nationwide truce might be arranged. The National Urban Peace and Justice Summit, as it was called in Kansas City, drew members of the Bloods, Crips, Vice Lords, and Disciples together for the first time and promised to put an end to the spiral of violence that has engulfed many city neighborhoods during the past decade.

The Mayor of Kansas City, Emanuel Cleaver, welcomed the participants at a buffet breakfast. Ben Chavis, executive director of the National Association for the Advancement of Colored People, pledged to support their work in extending the truce across the country. Carl Upchurch, the organizer of the summit and himself a former gang member, said that a main goal of the meeting was to find economic alternatives to crime and ways to rebuild inner-city neighborhoods. Gang members talked among themselves and reportedly blamed the media "for the public's bad image of gangs."[3]

I suppose there could be something to the claim that gangs have been misunderstood. Sociologist Joan Moore argues that we hold many unpleasant ideas or stereotypes about gangs, and that these images have a powerful effect on what we propose to do about "the gang problem." Moore says that when we think of gang members today we imagine beings who are "violent, drug- and alcohol-soaked, sexually hyperactive, unpredictable, confrontational, drug-dealing criminals." Gang members, she says, are supposed to be black or Latino, and their groups are thought to flourish in the slums of cities where there are poor and powerless neighbors on whom they prey. Gangs are popularly believed to be "all bad, and bad in the same kinds of ways. If it were proven beyond a doubt that one particular gang did not deal crack today, it would be expected to sell crack tomorrow."[4] No good is expected to be found in gangs.

I think there is merit in what Moore says. Absent the threat provided by a foreign bogeyman such as the former Soviet Union, gangs have become the nightmare of choice in our national closet. They bedevil us and make our best efforts at passing along our culture to a new generation look inept. At the same time, we *are* comfortable with our discomforting ideas about gangs, and there probably is not much that can dissuade us from holding these ideas or acting as if they were true. Moore acknowledges that sometimes gang members do bad things, but youths not affiliated with gangs do the same bad things. However unpleasant gangs may be, Moore believes that the truth about gangs is more complex than the simple pictures that we insist on carrying around in our heads. I think she is right.

It is harder to accept the idea that all the fear and hard feelings we have for gangs were planted in our empty heads by the media. Indiscriminate killing and drug dealing cannot be dismissed as poor fiction authored by sloppy reporters and aggressive editorial writers with nothing else to do and no one else to badger. Pre-paid funerals and drive-by shootings are not figments of our imagination. Crack houses and crack babies are real, and I assure you that they look every bit as horrid and pathetically lost in person as they do on television.

It is true that adults engage in sloppy thinking from time to time and are capable of making demons out of persons who are different from themselves. Nevertheless, no one's imagination is so overheated or their mind so filled with nasty dust that they would not recognize the death and betrayal of a generation when it hit them this hard. The real question is not whether such horrible things happened, but whether adults are willing to undo some of the bad things they helped to build or managed to ignore for so long.

Frederic Thrasher's Ghost

Any assessment of what we know and do not know about gangs in this century must begin with Frederic Thrasher. He was a sociologist at the University of Chicago earlier in this century and the first person to study gangs in a comprehensive way. His pioneering research on 1,313 Chicago gangs during the 1920s remains the standard against which subsequent work on the subject usually is judged.[5] No one who does research on gangs today fails to cite his famous study or to draw on his characterizations and explanations of gang behavior.

I confess there were times during interviews with gang members that I imagined that Thrasher's ghost was rattling around the room. I wondered how Thrasher might have felt as he pored over the stories brought to him by his research assistants, just as I was trying to make sense of the stories being told to me. You ask the same questions time after time in the hope that something important does not escape your attention. You fret endlessly about missing some vital insight or piece of information. You try to balance your excitement with discovering something new and different with the realization that any mistake you make may well have severe consequences for the persons with whom you are talking. All of this, I imagine, must have gone through Thrasher's head when he assembled and tried to make sense of all the information brought to him.

This does not mean that Thrasher went about his work with a completely open mind. His writing reveals a man who was pretty convinced about the harm done to youngsters by gangs. He also seemed certain that gangs flourished because the neighborhoods they were in and the adults in those places were not particularly nice. Children left to their own devices, Thrasher found, were apt to behave in less than congenial ways but also could display great devotion to each other. The environment in which those children lived and the adults who either ignored or influenced them did not help to steer youngsters into more conventional groups and ways of behaving. Nevertheless, gang members often found themselves enmeshed in the routines and customs of the ethnic peoples around them.

There were problems with his work. Foremost among them was Thrasher's ill-feeling about the foreign people and customs that shaped the world where gangs were found. Thrasher the scientist was heavily influenced by Thrasher the moralist who wanted to change the way gang members lived. Agency officials and business leaders who financed or followed his work closely were equally committed to fixing the world Thrasher called "Gangland." They may not have accomplished that goal, but they certainly offered the public a more complete picture of gangs and the slums where gangs were found than had been available previously.

In the end, that may be the best contribution that anyone writing about gangs can make. It certainly played a part in motivating me to sit through the hundreds of interviews that I conducted and in offering up as uncluttered and fair a view of the world of suburban gang members as could be presented. I understand better now how difficult it might have been for Frederic Thrasher to keep his job as scientist separated from his desire to make a better world. Thrasher actually may not have tried all that hard to keep the moralist and scientist in him from influencing each other. Nevertheless, he was really good at allowing both parts of himself speak to the six important questions that we still are trying to answer today.

What is a Gang and Who is in It?

These actually are harder questions to answer than one might imagine. For the longest time people were reluctant to look at gangs as a valid and viable form of human association. Gangs were recognized as creations of adolescent play groups, but something about the gang itself failed to qualify it as a "group" in its own right. Instead, a gang was called a "pack" or a "near group" or one of any number of other names that made it appear less effective and legitimate than an "institution" or "real group." Gangs were observed doing many of the same things that real groups did, but there was something about the way those actions were taken and the effect they had on their members or the wider community that made observers reluctant to attribute legitimacy to them.

There was an understandable, if perverse, logic to this naming game. The failure to assign value to a type of human association, no less than for another human being, allowed one to dismiss it or to treat it harshly. That was precisely the idea behind many so-called "gang intervention strategies" that social scientists or law enforcement officials often invoked to solve "the gang problem."

We have made some progress in how we name gangs. I think it fair to say that most academic writers today view gangs as one of many groups that youngsters may join. You will find us making comparisons, for instance, between gangs and athletic teams or families. This does not mean that social scientists believe that gangs are the same as families or athletic teams any more than we believe that contemporary youth gangs are really criminal syndicates. It means only that we find striking parallels between gangs and other more conventional types of groups.

Other observers of gangs are less kind. They still view gangs as primitive or corrupt enterprises with little or no redeeming social value. Perhaps that is why we still put so much emphasis on programs and policies whose effect would be to eradicate gangs or to separate young persons from gangs.

Our view of gang members also has changed, but not for the better. Early observers of youth gangs usually spoke of gang members as delinquents and troublemakers. These impressions were tempered by the fact that most gang members eventually "matured out" or left gangs as they grew older and assumed more conventional adult roles like "husband", "parent", and "employee." I think that gang members today are viewed more harshly. I have heard or read them referred to as drug dealers, criminals, murderers, and even "urban terrorists."

There is no doubt that some gang members are criminals, have murdered people, and do sell drugs. One should be reminded, as Joan Moore has said, that not all gang members are equally deserving of these labels and that youngsters who are not in gangs often are. The point is that contemporary gang members are being judged more severely than their predecessors were.

We call them nastier names in part because they do nastier things and frighten us more than gang members of an earlier age did. Furthermore, the boundary lines for gang membership have expanded. Children as young as eight or nine years of age have been known to participate in gang activities, and gang membership can persist well beyond the age of twenty.

Not as many gang members "mature out" as was once the case. They fail to leave their gang for a variety of reasons. Their inability to grow easily or naturally into more conventional adult roles – becoming a parent, spouse, or worker in any traditional sense – makes it more difficult for them to find alternatives to a life in gangs and easier for them not to try.

There is one last change in the young people who become gang members today that deserves special recognition. It was once the case that only boys were gang members. Girls might be part of an auxiliary group that was bound to a particular boys gang, but they had no distinct organizational identity. That no longer is the case, and it probably has not been true for longer than most of us know. Many gangs today are composed exclusively of girls, though they are not so numerous as boy gangs. Girl gangs also tend to be less violent and business-minded than their male counterparts. Still, they are out on the streets and they are active.

Girl gangs probably can be found today in most large cities. While we do not know much about them, it is thought that there are more of them because girls have fewer restraints on where they go and with whom they spend their time today than was once the case. They have more freedom and, as a result, they have begun to behave like the boys who live in their neighborhood.

I did not speak with any older gang members, but I certainly was told about them. From what I learned it appears that their number is not large. Nevertheless, they tend to remain involved in their gangs as leaders or suppliers of the narcotic substances that younger gang members sell. In the case of one gang, these older members were said to have taken some of this money and invested it in legitimate business enterprises.

I had a great deal of exposure to younger children who were flirting with the idea of becoming a gangbanger or who actually had been operating on the fringes of their neighborhood gang. Thrasher found that gangs emerged from the organized "play groups" of adolescents. Contemporary gangs in the suburbs also grow naturally from play groups composed of children. They are drawn to gang involvement by their older siblings and friends in the neighborhood. Their introduction to the ways of gangbanging and drug dealing is gradual and is designed to allow would-be gang members or "wannabes" to decide how much involvement they want and how quickly they want it.

The youngsters who are the driving force behind suburban gangs today are not very different from those Thrasher first identified in inner-city slums. They are teenagers. They may be more aggressive than many of their peers, or they may have learned to behave that way in order to look like competent gang members. The effect, in any case, is the same. They appear tough and wise to the way of the streets. They carry more money on their person than any teenager could possibly need. They may distinguish themselves by the way they dress and speak, but this is not always so.

In most other ways, they do not seem terribly different from teenagers who are not gang members. Some are quick and smart. Others appear less so. Some are engaging. Others are sullen and withdrawn. They are, as I already noted, teenagers.

Girls at every age seemed well informed about gangs, though not so well informed as boys of the same age. Gang membership for girls peaked in the early teen years. At no time did girl gangs fight as much as boy gangs, use weapons that were as dangerous, or become involved in as much criminal activity as did their male counterparts. Many more girls were attracted to boy gang members by virtue of the excitement that the boys brought with them and the money they flashed or spent on their "girlfriends."

I was struck by how natural and right it seemed to many girls that they accept such "presents." It became clear that girls gradually grew accustomed to giving something back to the boys who showered them with gifts or cash. A small number of girls in their teens had graduated into prostitution, though none of them or their friends acknowledged this fact. If their parents knew what they were doing, and it is hard to imagine that parents could not have suspected that something was going on, it was evident that this knowledge had little or no impact on their children's behavior.

Another element in becoming part of the gang member's world that I found particularly striking was what youngsters thought about their life in gangs. Frankly, they worried about the choices they were making a great deal more than I imagined they would. Most researchers lead one to believe that these youngsters adopt an identity as a gang member and then push on their merry way. I found that they were willing to talk about their fears.

While they might not have shared their concerns with many of their fellow gang members, individual youngsters clearly talked with their closest friends about the pressures they felt. Adolescents were not so smitten with the world of gangs or hooked by the quick money they made in it that they overlooked the dangers involved or the impact of their involvement on themselves and other persons. Suburban gang members in their teen years did not view gangbanging as a career and sometimes discussed their plans to pull away from their gang or described steps they already had taken to do so. Unlike younger children who openly shared fearful stories about having to kill a relative in order to escape from one's gang, teenagers knew that it was they and not their parents who were in the greatest danger and that leaving the life of a gangbanger was safer than remaining a part of it.

Although I found it interesting that a number of suburban gangs included white youngsters, I know that racially-mixed gangs in city neighborhoods probably have been around since the 1970s or 1980s. Of greater significance, I think, was the participation in suburban gangs of youngsters from stable middle-class families that have both parents living in the same household. I did not make a careful count of how many admitted gang members came from such families, but it was apparent from my conversations that a fair number did. Inasmuch as no previous piece of research on gangs with which I am familiar has made note of the involvement of such youngsters, I am inclined to conclude that gangs may be attractive to a variety of young persons for equally varied reasons. Gangs may serve as a substitute family for some youngsters or give less well-to-do youths a way to make money. The most vital service they render, however, may be to put young persons in contact with other teenagers at a time in their lives when developing greater independence and a more adult-like identity is really important.

Where are Gangs Found?

If I have accomplished nothing else in this book, I have squashed the idea that gangs are found only in slums or inner-city neighborhoods. Gangs, we see, are not found exclusively in cities. They will recruit members, bring their violence, and sell their drugs in the suburbs.

This may be less a surprise today than it was when I conducted my study of gangs in the Fairview School District. Newspaper and television news stories about gangs in suburbs have made their way to the public since that time. Still to be written are stories about gangs in small towns in rural areas in states such as Kansas and Minnesota. Gangs are operating in such places today. The news media simply have not yet figured it out or had it brought to their attention.

The significance of finding gangs in suburban towns cannot be overstated. It shows that areas around cities are not immune to the problems ordinarily associated with run-down neighborhoods in the middle of a ghetto or slum. Persons who live outside of cities have one less reason to think that they have walled themselves off from city people or the stresses and strains of city living. They also have one more reason to become involved in efforts to fix whatever is wrong in city neighborhoods that have gangs.

The discovery of gangs in suburbs is important for another reason. It tells us that our explanations or theories about gang behavior probably are overstated, if not altogether wrong. Earlier I noted that the name we use to label gangs suggests something about the policies and programs we will adopt to make gangs less threatening. Just as *what* we call a gang has implications for how we treat it or how we view gang members, *where* we expect to find gangs is supposed to tell us a great deal about the kind of human beings in them and the kind of morality they practice.

Frederic Thrasher and every researcher who followed him thought that only certain types of places had gangs. These places were in run-down, inner-city areas populated by minority groups who had little money and even less appreciation for conventional modes of behavior and speech. These neighborhoods also were thought to be "disorganized" places. When sociologists spoke of communities in this way they had in mind the kind of groups operating there and the kind of morality practiced by the residents.

Institutions and groups give a sense of order and direction to our lives. In areas that were thought to be disorganized, these social creations either were thought to be absent or ineffective. Churches, schools, neighborhood improvement associations, bowling teams, political parties, business leagues, fraternities and sororities, labor union headquarters, literary clubs, and dozens of other kinds of organizations that can be found operating in many healthy places were not supposed to work well or at all in areas that have gangs, or so it usually was assumed. The kinds of roles that individuals play in viable places also were not supposed to be found where gangs are operating. People would not be seen holding a variety of jobs, and local businessmen were not expected to live in the immediate area. Mothers would not be observed taking leisurely strolls with their infant children. Fathers would not teach their sons and daughters how to play baseball. Older residents would not admonish children when they misbehaved. Those who felt free to walk the streets at night were not the kinds of individuals that one would want dropping in for a visit.

This is part of what sociologists had in mind when they referred to areas with gangs as being "disorganized," but they also worried about the kind of morality revealed in the customs and values of persons living in a particular spot. In places like Thrasher's Gangland, the morality being practiced was not of a sort that conventional people would admire. Neighborhoods with gangs were considered too rough and foreign in their temperament for most Americans. It was assumed that those living in these areas would have to change important parts of their culture before gangs would disappear or become less threatening.

The spots where researchers and reporters typically looked for gangs were more like the disorganized places imagined by sociologists, and these places were inner-city slums occupied by immigrants. Gangs invariably were found there. Researchers and reporters did not look for gangs in cozy and generally quiet suburban neighborhoods. It was assumed that suburbs did not have the right kind of morality and unkempt social groupings to spawn gangs.

Some sociologists did not agree with this assessment of inner-city neighborhoods. They studied a number of neighborhoods in different cities and found these places to be far more orderly and sound than most persons would imagine.[6] Gangs might appear in such places, but they were not so depraved or rapacious as was feared. Indeed, gangs were seen as helping to enforce a kind of morality in an area that worked well enough for those who lived there.

This was an important idea. All gangs might not be the same, and they could take on a different character depending on the kind of neighborhood in which they were found. Gangs in "disorganized slums" would behave worse, and they would not have the kind of community backing that gangs found in "stable slums" enjoyed.

We figured this out several decades ago, but not much was done with this idea until the latter 1970s when the most recent upsurge in gang activity occurred. By then, the nature of gangs seemed to have changed dramatically and for the worse. There was more violence, more illicit criminal activity, and more fear attached to contemporary gangbanging. No one paid too much attention to whether gangs in some city neighborhoods were less fearsome, violent, or drug sodden than gangs found in other city neighborhoods. Certainly, no one thought to look for gangs in places like the Fairview School District.

The towns and neighborhoods comprising the Fairview School District are nothing like inner-city slums. They look a great deal like suburban areas that are found in many parts of the country. Many of the homes and neighborhoods are quite nice and have white and black inhabitants with middle-class tastes and pocketbooks. Other parts of the school district have smaller but still comfortable homes that are occupied by working-class families or even relatively poor families. These different properties tend to be concentrated in specific towns, and there are more towns with modest dwellings than with handsome structures. Rental properties in the area hold a variety of tenants from different income groups, and these units are spread throughout the district. There are several shopping areas and some light industry in different parts of the area as well.

No one looking at the townships comprising the Fairview School District would think them a natural setting for youth gangs; but the gangs are there and they are active. If there is something in the geography or appearance of these townships that would dispose their younger inhabitants to form gangs, I fail to discern it. When I drive through the towns or walk down the streets it is hard for me to pick out signs of social disorganization or a flawed moral order.

I know that the population of some towns has changed a great deal. There are many more black inhabitants there than had once been the case, and more of them are less well-to-do than in earlier times. There are, to be sure, less attractive towns in the district; and the less prosperous towns have more black faces in evidence than white ones. Yet this alone tells us nothing, unless one is prepared to overlook much theorizing about gangs that puts them in areas quite unlike the ones I have described. One would have to argue now that there is something about an area being recently populated by black persons or being less than middle class that disposes its youngsters to build gangs. It is true that most gang members in the Fairview School District are black and most probably come from less well-to-do families. On the other hand, gangs can be found operating in every township, and they can have both white and middle-class black members. There simply is nothing in our theorizing about gangs to lead one to look for them in places like the Fairview School District.

I am forced to conclude that our theories about where gangs are found and why they are found in those places are wrong. The only place that Gangland ever really existed was in Frederic Thrasher's mind. All the researchers who faithfully followed the path he cut made the same mistake and were as lost as he was.

There is nothing about inner-city neighborhoods that makes them more susceptible to gangs and nothing about suburban towns that makes them impervious to the influence of gangs. The important issue is not where gangs are found. Apparently, gangs can appear and thrive quite nicely in markedly different communal settings. Nor is the kind of moral order reflected in areas where gangs are found a central issue. When places as different as inner-city slums and suburban townships have gangs, one must submit that either persons in both places share the same values and moral vision or that their unique views about what is right or wrong cannot tell us much about where gangs will develop.

I prefer the latter explanation. Still, I acknowledge that many people would be inclined to believe that the same moral debasement that they attribute to life in many inner-city neighborhoods has spread into the suburbs with the migration of less well-to-do minority groups to those places. From there it is only a short jump to the view that new minority residents somehow spread, or infected, the gang virus to youngsters who had been living in those towns for a long time. This is an appealing argument on many levels, but it does not take us especially far in understanding what was going on in the towns that were part of the Fairview School District.

Several black teachers and administrators who had worked in the district for a number of years made a special effort to tell me about the way white boys from different towns once defended their community's honor through fights and scuffles long before there were many black youngsters in the area. The period during which their towns and schools had gone from predominantly white to mostly black was difficult for everyone, and there were fights between black and white youngsters. In the view of these adults, however, the black adolescents were investing their new towns with the same sense of importance or group pride that had been exhibited by the white youngsters who had once lived there. What the black kids were doing today, these adults maintained, was no different from what the white kids had done in the past.

There was more than a hint of defensiveness in the voices of the black teachers who related this history to me. They clearly were embarrassed by the behavior of black youths that routinely brought cops to football and basketball games in search of fights between rival gangs. However defensive their story may have been, it was confirmed by other persons, and it made a lot of sense. White boys had created groups and routines through which they had expressed pride for their towns. These groups may not have been called gangs, but they behaved liked them in some ways. What black boys and girls built went way beyond anything previous residents had seen before. Newer black residents to the area had introduced new or at least different ways of doing things and looking at the world, but their creations contained elements of stories that earlier residents had written. How youngsters built and operated gangs in the uncharted territory called "the burbs" was an important part of their new story.

How are Gangs Organized?

How we imagine gangs often is at odds with what gangs actually are like. One way this becomes obvious is in the way we view and describe how gangs are organized. Frederic Thrasher alluded to gangs as a form of "collective behavior." Later writers referred to gangs as "collectivities" or "near groups," among other things.[7] Upon closer inspection, though, gangs were seen to be quite complex social creations that could take a variety of shapes and meet an equally broad array of needs for their members.

The age-graded set or clique of youngsters was the fundamental building block of gangs back in Thrasher's day and remains so in modern cities and suburbs. These blocks can be arranged in different ways. Some gangs consist of only one such clique. Other gangs possess several sets that are strung together into a single unit.

One should not push comparisons between gangs and other types or organizations too far, but those who study corporations would say that gangs have a "flat" organizational structure. If there are officers at all, the distance between them and regular members is not great and is influenced by all sorts of personal considerations. More often than not, decisions on matters great and small are reached jointly.

Relations *among* the sets of modern city gangs need not be particularly friendly. They may come to the aid of each other only on certain prescribed occasions such as a large gang fight or when drug dealing takes place. Most of the time they simply may not have a great deal to do with each other. Alliances *between* different gangs have been difficult to build and sustain over long periods of time. Disagreements and fights between gangs that are supposed to be on good terms are not uncommon.

Gangs in the Fairview School District possessed many of these traits.

Members were drawn from neighborhoods within each town. Younger children did not have to be recruited to join gangs. They simply made themselves available to the teenagers who already were part of the local gang and expressed their interest in becoming a member. Established gangbangers might involve younger children in some gang activities, but the introduction of new persons to a gang's routines was gradual and usually involved little pressure. Aspiring gang members spent much of their time with their fellow novices in no small part because they attended school together. Once outside of school the younger children might hang around the older boys, but that probably was the extent of their routine contact with the more experienced gang members. It should be recalled that many youngsters had brothers, cousins, and neighbors in the local gang, so that routine access to older members was all but guaranteed.

Gangs probably were the first voluntary organization to which many youngsters belonged.[8] Youngsters from the different towns could elect to join a gang or not, depending on their own assessment of what was important to them. Most probably did not join their local gang; but they remained on friendly terms with youngsters who did and might, under the right circumstances, "go down" with their fellow townsmen during a fight with another gang. Whatever else one might think about these groups, they usually did not intimidate youngsters from their own town. Insofar as bullying took place it ordinarily entailed bigger boys picking on younger or smaller children and did not involve attempts to force children into becoming a gang member. The absence of forced recruitment and the easy relations between gang members and other youngsters in the neighborhood appears to distinguish gangs in the Fairview School District from gangs in many inner-city neighborhoods today.

Gangs in the Fairview School District also were able to develop a loose confederation among themselves more easily than inner-city gangs are thought to do. The alliances they formed were brittle and shifted from time to time, but gangs from some towns had a history of being on relatively good terms with each other. In general, gangs from smaller towns tended to have good relations with the gangs from larger towns contiguous to their own. The same gangs had poorer relations with their counterparts in larger towns some distance from their own.

What Do Gangs Do?

What gangs do probably is more important in the public's imagination than how they are organized, make alliances, or recruit new members. After all, a picture of young men shooting automatic weapons at each other is more compelling than a diagram of their organizational genealogy. Indeed, it is just such images of gang members that informs much of what we believe about contemporary gangs and pushes us to treat them as a problem requiring a tough response.

Delinquent and dangerous behavior nearly always figure prominently in our understanding of what gangs are like. However important such behavior may be in regulating their lives and prompting us to act against them, it does not define everything that gang members do. Much of the time they keep each other company, party, and talk. They sometimes fight with each other. They like to distinguish themselves by wearing special clothing, creating little rituals familiar only to their members, giving their group a name, and claiming to represent some fine ideal or a particular part of the community in which they reside. In short, they behave in pretty conventional ways much of the time. It is what they do with those remaining pieces of time that unnerves the rest of us.

Some people argue that gangs are not as bad as they are portrayed in the media, because youngsters who are not in gangs often shoot each other, sell dangerous narcotics, and tear up neighborhoods. They also note that from time to time a whole gang may be blamed for something that its individual members did. The gang, as such, is not responsible for murdering, selling drugs, or committing mayhem, although some of its individual members may be.

There is some validity to these observations. Not every delinquent or conventional act undertaken by gang members carries with it the explicit approval of the group as a whole. On the other hand, some acts do require the collaboration of many, if not most, members of the gang. Furthermore, much is done with the tacit approval of the larger group, and other actions would not be initiated without it.

Thrasher and other researchers found that fighting was the only activity that routinely involved most members of the gang. The honor of standing up for one's group and neighborhood, no less than the dishonor of failing to take up arms in its defense, was shared by everyone. It was through such experiences that the gang's identity was established and became part of the area's character and routines.

The struggle against real or imagined enemies, Thrasher and others argued, plays an important part in the daily routines and folklore of the gang. It becomes even more important, perhaps, when the gang becomes involved in criminal activities, because the group always needs to remain vigilant. Individual members would not survive long or as well without the protection provided by their gang.

Gangs in the Fairview School District followed this tradition to a point, but they found ways to grant exemptions to members who had reasons to avoid a particular fight. A number of youngsters also told me how their groups limited the amount of violence that took place during fights. It did not seem that the different gangs lost any credibility in the eyes of their members or their opponents as a result of such actions. Some enemies, it appeared, were less loathsome in practice than they were in theory.

In many ways, though, the influence of the gang was felt by all the members and influenced the decisions they made. As I have argued elsewhere regarding the gang's influence on the commission of crimes, gangs may not cause crime "in the sense that they brought lawlessness to an otherwise law-abiding community." What gangs did was to make "more efficient and extensive those activities that were an accepted part of the area's unconventional or hidden economy. In this sense gangs did make crime a more serious or pronounced part of the community's routines and its residents' habits" and implicated everyone in its activities.[9]

If the world of gangs has changed at all in this century, it would seem that more gangs today are deeply involved in serious criminal activities than was once the case. The law breakers are younger. They are more likely to employ deadly force to maintain their business enterprises. Finally, much more of this business activity involves suppliers and customers who reside some distance from the gang's home territory.

The gangs in the Fairview School District certainly fit into this new world. Much criminal activity related to car theft, burglary, and drug dealing in their towns is organized by them or carried out through them. Not all members engage in these activities, and few do it all the time; but enough do. There is no doubt that gangs are bringing a lot of misery to towns in the Fairview School District. Thus far, however, they have not treated their neighborhoods or schools as harshly as many inner-city gangs have treated their own areas and institutions.

That they might behave differently from gangs in the inner city is an idea worth exploring in greater detail; and there is no better way to do this than to look at the way gangs behave in different school settings. Our understanding of what gangs do in schools has been shaped by the experiences of schools in large cities such as New York, Chicago, and Los Angeles. The picture emerging from these schools since the 1970s is frightening and suggests a world that is being torn apart. Indeed, it looks a great deal like the "disorganized" world that early sociologists described in their research.

Sometime during the early 1970s, apparently, gangs extended the practice of claiming sovereignty over neighborhoods in which their members lived to the schools found in those neighborhoods. Suddenly what once had been "neutral turf" became just another spot where gang rivalries, vendettas, and recruitment took place. An early chronicler of this story, Walter B. Miller, described gangs as "prowling the school corridors in search of possible rivals, and preventing orderly movement through the hallways." Gang fights, the intimidation of teachers and school personnel, the parading of gang "colors" or other identifying markers, the carrying of dangerous weapons, and the extorting of money from students and staff alike became part of school routines. These were schools, as author William Gale wrote in 1977, where the "principal never walked the halls alone."[10]

The situation in these schools did not improve during the 1980s. If anything, conditions grew worse. Ray Hutchison and Charles Kyle studied Hispanic street gangs in and around two Chicago high schools and found that these groups had a "pernicious presence" in the schools. Gangs effectively controlled much of what took place and did not take place in classrooms and large portions of the school building. They ran "extensive and lucrative drug trafficking" operations in the school, recruited members, and intimidated and beat students in school, on school grounds, and on the blocks surrounding the school site. Students listed gang activity as an important reason for dropping out of school, and administrators took steps to transfer students who were at risk from attack by gangs.[11] Adults were still officially in charge of these schools, but it was gang members who actually determined much of what passed for a daily routine.

This certainly was not the case in the Fairview School District. Both real and aspiring gang members made their presence felt in a variety of ways. Students from different gangs fought, flashed signs, wore their colors, and, in some cases, sold drugs in school buildings or on school grounds. Only in the junior high school, however, did gang members come close to undermining the authority of school staff and make it difficult to conduct classes in an orderly way. The district had a gang problem, but it was not nearly as severe as the problems created by gangs in big-city schools.

The reasons why most schools in this district were not disrupted by gangs are not difficult to discern. Most younger children attended school in the towns where they lived, and the gang members they usually saw were those who belonged in that town. There were children who pretended to be from rival gangs in each elementary school, but they did not create an environment in which students could not learn and teachers could not teach. Youngsters who belonged to gangs other than the one most represented in the school made a sincere effort not to make their gang affiliation known to other students.

Students from different towns and rival gangs did not come into routine contact in the schools until they reached the junior high school. Frankly, neither students nor school staff were prepared for this situation, and they did not respond well to problems created by having so many gangs bumping into each other on a daily basis. Teachers and administrators ignored the presence of gangs in their school and were content to suspend as many students as was necessary to create the impression that they knew what they were doing.

Students spoke of all the turmoil in the junior high school in strong terms. There were some students who were disgusted with the situation, but did not know what could be done about it. There were other students who rather enjoyed all the noise and trouble they made. Still others recognized that their involvement in ongoing fights with rival gang members was stupid and potentially dangerous. They were looking for a way out of the situation, but they, too, were not at all sure what could be done. In the meantime, they continued playing the role of committed gangbanger.

By the time these youngsters graduated from the junior high school and moved up to the high school, they were either pretty tired or really full of themselves. The tired ones remained active in their gangs and could be counted on to jump into a fight at the high school, if someone from their gang were being insulted or assaulted. The ones who came to the high school looking for trouble and trying to establish reputations for themselves as tough guys found both. Older, more established gang members quickly asserted their authority, however, and they kept most of their younger peers in line much of the time. Few students brought weapons to school, and few "hard" drugs such as cocaine were sold on the campus.

It is not supposed to be this way. Everything we know about gangs in inner-city schools indicates that by the time gang members enter high school they are supposed to be meaner and less restrained. Why did this not happen in the Fairview School District? Why did gang members behave better in the high school than they had at the junior high school?

The answer, I think, is easy to figure out. Students came to understand that they had no place else to go. Everyone from different towns and rival gangs had a right to be at Fairview High School. They may not have liked that situation, but there was nothing that they could do to change it. They might have responded by fighting and selling drugs as they did on the streets, or they could learn to get along and keep the school from being torn up. They chose to restrain themselves and to behave better than they did on the streets or had acted at the junior high school. Pride in their gangs and a defense of their town's honor continued to be expressed at the high school, just as it once had been by white adolescents from each town in the district. The big difference was that black gang members did not carry on their rivalries, or business deals, with the same vigor or violence as they practiced on the street.

Gang members at the high school reasserted the tradition of treating schools as neutral territory, a place that could belong to everyone. It was hard work, and they did not succeed all the time. Nevertheless, they made their intentions clear every day and did behave much better than one might have expected.

What is the Gang's Relation to the Community?

It should be clear by now that not all gangs act identically and that there are differences in the way gangs in suburbs and cities behave. I suspect that the distinction between city and suburban gangs probably is not especially useful. However, it does help to account for what I found in the Fairview School District and what reporter Melinda Henneberger of the *New York Times* discovered about gangs in Yonkers, New York during the summer of 1993.[12] Much more important, I believe, would be a distinction between gangs in neighborhoods and towns that are comparatively stable and gangs in places that are not stable at all. These latter communities probably would be identified by sociologists as being "disorganized" and full of individuals with serious problems.

I raise this as an issue now because the way gangs behave in different settings tells us a great deal about their relations with other groups and residents in their community. It seems that gangs that have good ties to other local groups and to adults in their area behave in a more restrained way. They do not tear up their own neighborhood and do not intimidate the those who live there. Gangs that have poor ties to area groups and residents behave quite differently. They are much more likely to destroy property and to harass their neighbors. In short, they show no concern for the peace and well-being of the place where they live and the people who share that place with them.

The importance of community ties was noted first by Frederic Thrasher in his early study of Chicago gangs. Thrasher found that many gang members identified closely with their neighbors and frequently defended their neighborhood against outsiders. This antagonism extended to agencies and individuals who went into their neighborhood to make it a better place and their fellow neighbors more respectable. It even was directed toward local groups that made no room in their world for the boys in gangs. Area groups and organizations run by adults that did establish ties to the local boys fared much better.

Thrasher did not approve of the boys' relations with local adults whom he considered to be less than desirable characters. Ward politicians, tavern keepers, and residents who curried favor with gang boys, used their services and bought stolen goods from them, were thought to corrupt the boys. It would have been preferable, Thrasher thought, for the boys to become more involved with adults and organizations from outside their neighborhood. Only then, he believed, would gang boys see that they could be part of a larger, more conventional world hidden from their view by the sorry places and persons with whom they came into daily contact.

Researchers and reformers who followed Thrasher worried about the connection between gangs and their neighborhoods, and much money was spent during the 1960s to make gangs into conventional political and business organizations. These efforts did not work out well. Social scientists were more interested, however, in nailing down one or another feature of gang life so that they could make general statements regarding gang organization and behavior or create theories about gang members as juvenile delinquents.

Our desire to play at being real scientists had serious consequences. It took our attention away from the communities where gangs were found and the groups that might have effectively restrained them. Sociologists, psychologists, therapists, and criminal justice experts became more aware of how to manipulate gangs and their members. Furthermore, they encouraged everyone else to treat gangs as a disease that only would respond to the special medicine that real scientists could prescribe.

We learned from the experience of gangs in the Fairview School District that what happens in a community and its important institutions matters a great deal. Gang members often behaved poorly and committed dangerous acts, and they did not universally revere the towns where they lived or treat respectfully all the children and adults who lived there with them. Nevertheless, there was something going on in these towns and in some schools that made most gang members more mindful of what they were doing and the impact that their actions had on other persons. Something stopped them from acting like gangsters and killers.

Even among the most committed gang members there was an understanding that there were limits beyond which they should not step and a price that they eventually would pay for behaving as they did. I can make some informed guesses as to where they acquired this understanding, and all my hunches take me back to the friends and family members, ministers, teachers, and other sane adults who occupy the gang members' world. I can say with complete certainty that their understanding did not come from a sociologist, psychologist, or any other slick expert pushing an open hand and an emptier head. Nor did it come from cops who stole their drugs and money, from movies and television shows that made gangs look noble, or from drugged-out parents and neighbors, lazy teachers, and the other incompetent adults who occupy the world of gang members.

Gang members in the Fairview School District behaved as they did because there were enough adults and organizations around to show young men and women pictures of what their lives could be like after gangs. I do not think the answer is a lot more complicated than that. Others are not so sure.

What Can We Do About Gangs?

Public officials, private agencies, scientists, and a host of other parties have tried many times and used a variety of techniques to make gangs go away or to choke off the supply of would-be gang members. Our interest in developing a cure for gangs is genuine, but evidence of our failures is overwhelming and all over the place. Gangs have not disappeared and, in fact, are appearing in communities where we have not seen them before. No one has made a count of the number of gangs in any one place over a long period of time, much less for the country as a whole. Had such a count been kept, however, I suspect that the number of gangs and gang members today would be unprecedented in our history. Whatever we did in the past to curtail gang activity simply did not work.

I fear that this situation will grow worse. A national criminal syndicate is being built by larger black and Latino gangs that have been involved in the drug trade for a long time. It was born in Kansas City in April 1993. This syndicate will employ many young men and women across the country, and it will invest some of its profits in legitimate businesses in the places where it is found.

The Bloods, Crips, Vice Lords, and Disciples who will build this syndicate will not be nicer for having become quieter. They will continue to sell drugs, and they will kill when the need arises. These national gangs will make and keep their truce, but it will extend only to these larger organizations.

The larger gangs will divide the nation into wholesaling territories and generally respect the boundary lines they have set for themselves. Transgressions and occasional lapses in good judgment will be handled quickly by the gangs themselves without much publicity. Local groups in different cities and towns will be free to kill their competitors. These smaller gangs never were important to the larger, national gangs anyway except as retail distributors for illegal narcotics. Thus, any losses among them will not be missed.

If gangs are not going away and tolerating their activities is not a viable option, then we will have to find new ways to limit the impact they have on us. Federal and state law enforcement officials will take care of the national syndicate. They finally will be able to use the racketeering and property confiscation laws available to them in ways that they were intended to be used. The use of such statutes against small gangs like those in the Fairview School District is unwarranted and a waste of time.

If federal and state officials do their job properly, it will leave local citizens to deal with gangs like those found in many cities and suburbs. Given our record in such matters, it is unlikely that we will do much that has not been tried before. Community leaders will take steps to discourage adolescents from joining gangs. Youngsters already involved in gangs will be lured from the violence and crime practiced by their peers. Their groups will be pursued aggressively by law enforcement agencies, and members who are not killed will be sent to jail for long periods of time.

It may be necessary and right to take these steps, but we should not be surprised when little good comes back to us because of these efforts. The record of success for such initiatives is poor. We will be reminded that attempts to eradicate gangs ordinarily fail and can make worse an already bad situation. Policies designed to wean youngsters from gangs in order to reduce their number also will fail. Gangs already are too well rooted in most communities and too important to the youngsters who are affiliated with them for such strategies to work.

There are persons who have thought a great deal more than I have about doing away with gangs. You can track them down and ask them what they think, or you can read their books and research papers as I have done. The weight of their ideas and the power of their scientific rhetoric are impressive. Unfortunately, after wading through all their stuff, you might well be uncertain about what can be done to curb gang violence and criminal ventures. In fact, you may be more confused.

They talk about strategies that are designed to help juvenile offenders learn how to be more reflective, or to make better moral choices, or to gain control over their emotions, and to solve problems without resorting to violence. They suggest programs that are intended to draw out the warmer and fuzzier parts of otherwise sullen and aggressive gang members. Youths, it is suggested, should be trained to be more thoughtful about other people, to listen better, and to use better communication skills. They will be asked as well to forget all those provocative hand signs and body markers that gang members use all the time.

Experts also propose that we try to help the families of delinquent youngsters cope more effectively with their troubled children. Once beyond the family, the attention of program designers turns to schools, recreational leagues, potential employers, community groups, and, of course, the police as potential helpers in the battle to win over or beat down gangs.[13]

There is no shortage of theories, research, and policies regarding what to do about gangs. In fact, there probably is more information than we can use profitably. Too many policies and theories about gangs, however, have yielded equivocal results once they were put into practice.

Many approaches to changing the behavior of gang members or delinquents seem to make a difference for awhile, but not so big a difference or for so long that anyone could say with confidence that he had discovered *the* answer to the gang problem. On the other hand, people have tried strategies that did little good but were introduced under trying circumstances, and this made it difficult to dismiss the effort as a total failure. The strategy might work better, it is suggested, if only it were tried again or with a slightly different twist.

Scientists and therapists really cannot tell us what will work in any definitive way for a long period of time. They can speak with slightly more authority about what seems to make matters worse. In this regard, it appears that trying to harass gang members or put their gang out of business serves only to stiffen their resolve and make them fight harder. Suppression, as I have already indicated, does not work.

Some things probably can be done to restrain gang members, but these strategies have not been introduced in any systematic way to communities with gangs. Instead, they emerge rather predictably from the way that many organizations and neighborhood groups run by adults carry out their normal routines. These enterprises often incorporate youngsters and tie them to work that sustains the community.

A few programs designed by reformers actually replicate the work of neighborhood groups and voluntary associations. Unfortunately, project directors often do not appreciate how much their work mimics what already is occurring naturally "in the field." They fail to see just how important the work of organizations such as churches or voluntary associations can be in shaping the behavior of gang members and in making the group less threatening. Sociologists call these organizations "mediating structures" because they literally negotiate paths that we can safely follow to reach a larger world occupied by strangers and faceless bureaucracies. Thrasher first described the work of such groups, but he did not take it seriously because of his disdain for the individuals running the ethnic clubs, taverns, and political organizations found in Gangland. Subsequent reformers and scientists repeated his error, or they tried to make gangs into conventional organizations.[14]

I learned of the importance of "mediating structures" for gang members by observing what went on in the Fairview School District and by talking with gang members. Many times they spoke of gangs as the only important "mediating structure" in their lives. In so doing, they became powerful advocates for sound families, effective community groups, and the imposition of limits on student conduct. The presence or absence of such influences in their lives has a telling effect on the nature and extent of gang activity. Stable communities dampen gang activity and promote conventional adult behavior.

Gangs help to build young human beings every bit as much as families, churches, schools, and neighbors do. It is important, then, to ask ourselves what it is about gangs that makes them such powerful shapers of young persons' lives. I am hardly the first to wonder about this. On the other hand, I think that the children of the Fairview School District provided me with some interesting, or at least different, ideas on this subject. These same children also helped me to understand a little better how it was that our grown-up culture does not provide many good ways for some children to become more conventional adults. Important clues to how we build our culture are to found in the workings of gangs and the ways that gangs help to build young human beings.

What Gangs Teach Us about Making Human Beings

It is not particularly hard to make a baby, and there is much about the experience that gives great pleasure. It is a lot more difficult to make a human being. The process takes substantially longer. There are more by-standers watching or offering advice. There are many more ways to do it right or do it wrong. It is difficult to know when you are finished. When you do finish, it may be years before you are certain that it was any good. Worst of all, by the time you figure out that it *was* good, you may be too old to try again or too tired to care.

In the making of human beings at certain places and times, gangs are one of the groups that watch the progress being made by young persons and offer them advice. They teach children the difference between right and wrong. They let youngsters know where the boundary line between themselves and the outside world is set, and they give youths a sense of themselves in relation to the other persons in the group. Gangs show children how to become a particular kind of human being, and they present youths with opportunities to practice being that kind of person. Gangs reward youngsters for their effort and accomplishments, and gangs let youths know when they have become the type of person that fits in the world where gangs are found.

Gangs are democratic to a fault. They will train minority children and children with blond hair and blue eyes with equal vigor and effectiveness. They attract youngsters from middle-class backgrounds as readily as they draw in children from working-class or lower-class families. On the other hand, we find that gang membership for many youngsters is problematic. They often enjoy the idea of gangbanging more than they like the respon-sibility of being a gang member.

They find drug dealing to be scary, dead-end work. It is only slightly less so when youngsters do it as a group. Felix Padilla showed us that drug dealing does not pay particularly well and that it exacts an emotional toll on the child who does it. He was right. Now we know just how widely these views are held by youngsters and how quickly they come to recognize the precariousness of their situation. Few see themselves staying with this kind of work for an indefinite period of time. They know it is dangerous and that they can be killed doing it. The money may be good, but it is not that good.

Gang members, we know now, often are reluctant warriors, and their gangs can use violence in a far more discriminating way than is commonly thought. They are mindful of the threat that their work and play pose to the neighborhoods where they live and to their families. They could disrupt schools more than they do, and they learn that such behavior wins comparatively little for them. A gang is important to its members, but it is not so important that most youngsters would give up their life to honor or serve it.

Gangs do not give meaning to a youngster's life, but they certainly offer ways in which youngsters can build a meaningful life for themselves and with persons their own age. That is why gangs are so important to young persons and why it is folly to try to destroy gangs. One might as well try to destroy the youngster himself. That you or I might not like the kind of youngsters produced with the help of gangs is in one sense irrelevant and in another sense quite important to the making of a gangbanger.

Our liking or disliking of gangs and the way they make a human being is irrelevant for the same reason that our attitude toward most other ways of making a human being in this country is irrelevant. To put it plainly, we adults do not see the building of healthy, emotionally sound, well-informed, and competent human beings as *the* central project of our lives. We have lost sight of the kinds of persons it is important for a society to make, if it is to work well.

Instead, we indulge ourselves by searching for a better, fuller, more satisfying personal identity. We fret endlessly about our own and others' self-esteem. We imagine the pursuit to be self-validating, and by our example we encourage others to view such behavior as socially responsible. Gang members have learned that lesson all too well, and we are all the poorer for it. We have left them, and our own children, too alone. I believe that Edwin Delattre is right when he says, "There is something of the coldest spirit of our age in this . . . presumption that benevolence consists in leaving our children to their own devices, as though ignorance and divorce from the human heritage were identical with the achievement of autonomy."[15]

Children, particularly children facing many real hardships, cannot be expected to take seriously our declarations of caring and warnings about the harm they do to themselves, if they see adults as weak, ineffectual, and unengaged in their lives. Too many youngsters see adults in that way. Gangs introduce children to adult responsibilities and concerns first as play and then as work. They give children an opportunity to achieve mastery in these endeavors. It does not matter that the behavior and values being extolled are, in their most extreme expression, inherently dangerous and ultimately corrupting. The behavior and values work well enough and long enough to imprint on youngsters a way of relating to each other and to the larger world that helps some of them make the difficult passage from childhood into adulthood a bit less problematic.

On the other hand, our dislike for the ways in which gangs build human beings helps to keep gang membership a valuable part of a youngster's identity. Gangbangers take satisfaction from our objections to their behavior and comfort from our inability to exercise much authority over them. They appear competent and untouched by the demands that others would put on them. I am acquainted with a number of adults who would enjoy such a feeling and for whom the appearance of competence and independence will be about as close as they are likely to get to the real thing. It is no surprise that many youngsters in gangs treat our objections to them as a source of pride and a reaffirmation of their accomplishments.

This is what gangs enable youngsters to do, if only in a limited and potentially destructive way. It also is why gang members seem to know more about building an identity for themselves through group work and play than do many adults who are unable to work together effectively and are self-indulgent to the point of damaging themselves. A gang offers its members opportunities to build an identity and to invest their lives with meaning through their collaboration with other youngsters in serious tasks. It does so more regularly and with greater effectiveness than do most of the other groups and institutions run by adults with which gang members come into routine contact.

None of this is to say, of course, that gangs ultimately do a good job of building a human being. The children and adolescents who spoke with me made it abundantly clear that they had serious concerns about the type of person they saw themselves or their peers becoming. They were frightened by the violence associated with gangs. They were aware of the corrupting influence of drugs both for the quick money they made selling crack cocaine and for the debilitating effects their "product" had on the adults who bought and used it.

Whatever good might have come from the preparation offered to youngsters by gangs was swallowed up by the harm gangs required their members to do and the quickness with which gang life unfolded and drew in young persons. Few adults are willing or able to assume the kinds of power over life and death claimed by many gang members almost as a birthright. It is absurd to think that youngsters would be able to deal effectively with the consequences of holding such power.

Once young persons in the Fairview School District took the time to think about what they were becoming and doing to others, they realized that they had been stretched well beyond their limits. They were not so competent as they had been led to believe, and they were trying to cram too much hard living into too little time. Many of them wanted to back away from gangbanging and were trying to do just that. Other youngsters were less certain about what course their lives should take. Gang membership put in bold relief the necessity for making such important decisions, but it gave them few alternative paths from which to choose and little time in which to do the choosing. We should not be surprised that many of their decisions were poorly informed and hastily made.

It takes a long time to make such important decisions. Whatever a human being has in himself to become, Beryl Markham has told us, "comes to light, not in one flamboyant hour, but in the ledger of his daily work."[16] We build an identity, one piece at a time, over the course of a lifetime. We invest life with meaning through our labors and our collaboration with other beings in important works, not just serious works like drug dealing. None of this comes easily or quickly.

These youngsters learned that they could not shop for an identity like they shopped for gold chains and designer clothes. Meaning in their life was not to be found through the purchase and display of trinkets or the pursuit of another exciting moment. It was to be hammered out on mean streets and through hard and dangerous work. They saw this and did not like it.

They needed more time, as J. Glenn Gray has said, "to acquire a self to know." It is because young persons "have not yet a conception of their powers and limitations," and thus "no stable character as a center for experience," that Gray thinks they stumble so often and hard along the way to building an identity.[17] It is no different for adults, even for those of us who work hard and are fortunate. We simply have learned how to stumble less often and to mask our bruises a little better. I came to understand that this process is much harder for many youngsters who belong to gangs. They come with less padding and carry fewer bandages.

The real surprise, perhaps, was not that so many youngsters left to their own devices had a hard time becoming competent teenagers and adults, but that so many probably would enjoy some success at it despite all the barriers thrown in front of them. While this would not be easy for them to do, it was not impossible either. The reason why was not hard to uncover, but it required one to let go of the idea that all gang members were bad all the time and in the same ways.

In the 1960s, sociologist David Matza said that gang members drifted in and out of delinquent activities. He spoke of how youngsters created a subculture of delinquency inside the conventional world run by adults. Young persons could be part of the larger world even as they stood in opposition to some of the standards practiced in it.[18] In fact, being a gangbanger could be seen as a strategy used by young persons to negotiate their way into the more conventional world run by adults.

This idea made a lot of sense to me. Youngsters from the Fairview School District spoke often of how they passed in and out of the drug trade or found ways to avoid certain fights. They made and carried out plans to back away from their career as a gangbanger. They held jobs in the regular economy even as they sold drugs. They stayed in school even though they mocked or ignored their fellow students who were working hard. They tried to keep their drug dealing from their parents, and some willingly gave their parents money in order to help out the family.

Academic persons like myself carry on heated arguments about how well or poorly gangs and gang members are integrated into our more conventional world. The current view on this matter is that gang members are almost entirely cut out of conventional society and depend on their gangs for social and economic support that they cannot find anywhere else. We think of gang members today as being more violent and more committed to illegal schemes to make money because they have rejected the conventional parts of our society and are not constrained by anyone. Involvement in gangs is one way that they are supposed to have adapted to the painful reality of having no hope or roots in the world that most of us take for granted.[19]

This thesis is popular, in part, because it fixes gang membership in that broad category of lost human beings called "the underclass." Persons in the underclass are thought to endure problems that are like those faced by gang members. They are seen exhibiting similar pathologies and probably face the same barriers to breaking from the miserable circumstances they share with gang members who reside in our nation's central cities. The primary difference between gang members and other persons in the underclass is that gangbangers are predators.

It is convenient to think of gang members in this way. There also is more than a little evidence to back up our impressions that gang members may have become the sharp-edged vanguard of the underclass. Appealing as it may seem, this assessment of contemporary gangbangers does not offer us much help in understanding the youngsters described in this book. These were suburban youngsters. They attended school. Many of them held part-time jobs in legitimate businesses. They had dreams about escaping from the life they knew, and gangs were part of the life from which they wanted to escape. Some were succeeding.

Observers of contemporary gangs would not recognize these youngsters. I also fear that social scientists like myself may contribute to the harm already being done to these youngsters by portraying them as alien creations. It becomes too easy to dismiss them or, perhaps, to treat them as an enemy when we have grown accustomed to thinking of them as outsiders.

My position is different. I do not view gang members as being permanently lost from our society or as rejecting many of the customs and values that we hold dear. Gang members, it seems to me, stand apart from the larger world but are trying to find a way to fit in it.[20] How gang members think of themselves and what they do complement what goes on in the larger society, even though there is much about gangbanging that hurts our society and is unflattering to the gang members. In an important sense, what I have done in this book is to show how gangs and gang members manage to coexist with the larger, more conventional society run by adults.

What Gangs Teach Us About Making a Culture

You may recall the young man named Tony who could not "see the logic" in the way local boys from the same town divided their loyalties between their municipality and different gangs from Los Angeles. It made no sense to him. The real surprise for me was not that the whole arrangement was confusing, but that it worked as well as it did. Apparently, it made sense to the youngsters who had constructed the arrangement, and that is really what mattered.

My job as a social scientist and author is to make sense of how other persons make sense of their world. This is not an easy chore. There are two tricks that anyone can use, however, to make the figuring out a little easier. First, one has to understand that there are many possible ways for individuals to build a relatively coherent and workable world for each other. Second, one has to understand that no single way of building a social world is inherently better or worse than any other.

This latter point is especially hard for some of us to accept, and I understand why. No one expects you to forget who you are and the life you live when you visit someone else's world. Indeed, your own experiences provide you with an important point of reference. The trick is not to assume that *your* reference point should be *their* reference point.

It is fortunate that human beings do not use every means available to them to create a social world that makes sense. We tend to imitate each other, and this cuts down the number and variety of ways that we use to impose a sense of order on to an unstructured social universe. Ordinarily, we also prefer the social world we know, or at least we are comfortable enough with it that we are reluctant to change often or dramatically.

The truth of this observation notwithstanding, one need not approve of the different ways that people use to build a coherent social world. Although I see merit in being tolerant of others' customs, at least until they bang hard against my own, I do not think that one need embrace these alien ways as much as be intellectually engaged by them. You need to determine just how different or similar someone else's customs are from your own and how their way of life folds into your own or rubs it raw. If you can do this, then you will be able to make better sense of how other people make sense of their world.

The way of life pursued by gangbangers is different from the one I knew as a youngster, and it certainly has little in common with the life I lead as a middle-aged university professor. Nevertheless, these youngsters were able to understand what I was talking about, and they were able to communicate their view of the world clearly and with considerable feeling. I did not have to share their life in order to understand how they made sense of their world, any more than they had to live with me in order to make themselves understood. We had enough in common to be able to communicate with each other, to articulate the differences between ourselves, and, most important, to share each other's company without coming to blows.

Herein laid the secret to how gangs and adults were able to tolerate each other in school and out in the neighborhoods. It was through nothing more dramatic than my conversations with them that I came to understand how they make sense of their world and how that world fits into my own. Put simply, *we try to ignore each other even when we should not.*

This may not sound particularly dramatic, but it is no less true or important for being dull. I will try to explain myself in a more detailed way, but the truth is that everything that I say after acknowledging the good and bad effects of ignorance is mere academic window-dressing. It may be thought-provoking, but it is still window-dressing.

I discovered that the culture, or subculture, of gangs fit in these towns and schools by not being too intrusive. The use of the term "culture" is not at all misplaced or too high-sounding. Gangs created a particular view of the world for their members and put it into practice. The creation of a worldview by any collection of human beings is vital work, and the fitting of that worldview into the ways in which persons conduct their daily lives is their culture.[21] In the case of the Fairview School District, a gang or delinquent subculture found sufficient time to develop and room to maneuver.

We know that the subculture of gangs had a great presence in the towns and schools of the Fairview School District. This finding alone would have surprised most inhabitants of the suburbs, who made this research worthy of being published by somebody. However, this was not the most interesting feature of the gang subculture. Far more interesting and important, I think, was the fact that the "great presence" of gangs in the Fairview School District was not known to everyone, and was barely acknowledged by some persons who were aware of its existence.

Gangs were much more important and visible to children and adolescents than they were to adults. Though there certainly were exceptions to this rule, gangs and gang members did most anything they wanted to do, when and where they wanted to do it, without much supervision or interference by adults. This was apparent in the neighborhoods where gangs were found, but it was especially obvious in the schools.

This was so not because gang members did more in the schools than they did on the streets but for the simple reason that they were under much closer adult supervision in the schools. Whatever we say, then, about the way in which the subculture of gangs fit into the conventional world of the school would be even more true out in the neighborhoods and towns where the gangs originated. In the neighborhoods, gangs carried out their activities with even less supervision by agents of the grown-up culture that they simultaneously fought and tried to enter.

The gang subculture, within the context of the school, parallels the culture endorsed by adults who are supposed to operate the site. These two cultures do not clash so much as bump. Moreover, the bumping happens in ways that allow adults to carry on many of their routines and to ignore the influence that gangs have in the school.

The subculture of gangs makes its presence felt in schools in much the same ways as the so-called "peer culture" does. Youngsters generally work hard to subvert school routines, stretch school rules, and test the limits of their teachers' patience. This is immensely aggravating to adults, but it is an effective and safe way for young persons to learn how to manipulate a complex organization and to challenge, however symbolically, the influence of adult authority on their lives. The significance of the gang subculture is that it is an exaggerated, better organized, and meaner version of the "peer culture" that operates in all schools to varying degrees.

The impact of the gang subculture sometimes seems more important than mere bureaucratic guerrilla warfare, however. It is as if the gang subculture were part of the school's curriculum. Many of those who write about educational matters, particularly those with a more liberal political perspective, speak of schools as having a "hidden curriculum."[22] They see schools as having all types of nasty biases built into the way they train children. There are racial biases, gender biases, and social class biases, to name just three of the more obvious candidates. These biases are thought to find expression in almost everything that goes on in schools. Yet the influence of this "hidden curriculum" is supposed to be so deeply embedded in school routines that most of the time we hardly notice it is there. While I am not so certain about the presence of these biases in schools, I have witnessed the presence of the gang subculture and its impact on school routines.

There is another noteworthy feature of the "peer culture" and the way it operates, at least in comparison to the gang subculture. Although it is the case that the "peer culture" practiced by students can be aggravating and silly, it usually can be accommodated within the school. Teachers may shrug their shoulders and principals may shake their head over the youthful exuberance of their charges, but they also try to capture that energy and channel it into clubs or teams that bring peace and fame to the school. Gang members may participate in school activities such as these, but their group cannot be readily accepted because it challenges too openly the administration of the school by adults.

This challenge to their adult caretakers notwithstanding, many elements of the gang subculture can be tolerated within the school setting. I found that gang members and school staff could live with each other satisfactorily, even though they sometimes had to work at it pretty hard or close their eyes to each other's mistakes and insults. A favorite strategy of school staff was to avoid reporting incidents involving gang members or, as the youngsters stated, to avoid identifying an incident as having anything to do with gangs.

In larger school districts with more than one junior or senior high school, another strategy adopted by school staff is to transfer troublesome gang members to another school. It bears noting that these same devices are used when problems arise with students who are not gang members. Thus, school officials are able to deal with many problems instigated by gang members in the same way they would with any other student. This makes it easier for them to ignore in any official way that their school may have a problem with gangs.

Gang members and their followers also worked at times to make gangs less threatening in the Fairview School District. This was less evident at the junior high school, but there the adults in charge worked overtime to ignore the influence of gangs. Gang members at the high school, on the other hand, refrained from making their presence too obvious. They fought members of opposing gangs, but they rarely identified themselves as gang members when they did this. They also provided the adults who ran the school with explanations for the fights that did occur. It was said that fights were initiated because students made unkind remarks about someone's family, friends, or town. School teachers and administrators accepted these explanations, or at least they were willing to pass the explanations along to their superiors as part of an official account of the disruption that took place. In some sense, they had no choice but to accept these explanations. Students and teachers had first used and heard them in the elementary schools. By the time students reached high school, few people outside of the Superintendent's office doubted that these explanations were true.

Some gang members at the high school also made it easier for themselves to blend in with their fellow students by doing passable and even outstanding academic work in their classes. They did not sell drugs often or at all during the school day, and they avoided wearing clothing that would identify themselves as gang members. This behavior made them more anonymous and protected their identity as gangbangers; but it also kept them in school and helped to prepare them to move into a more conventional world.

It was through such concessions that gang members and school staff were able to reach tacit agreements about the ongoing presence of gangs and gang activity in the schools. Gang members did not have to tear away at the official school culture. They only had to nudge it aside from time to time or tuck it away in a safe corner of their daily routine. Teachers and administrators were able to keep all established school routines intact and to maintain the appearance of having the school well under control.

This is the way gangs struck a bargain with officials in the Fairview

School District. The relation between gang members and school personnel in other districts, and here I am talking about inner-city districts, is a lot less congenial. In these other districts, gangs might be portrayed as having established a "counterculture" that sets out explicit codes of conduct and ways of thinking about schooling that actively compete with the standards and behavior promoted by adults in school buildings.[23]

Under these more challenging circumstances, it is better to view gangs as resisting more conventional models of student success. Gangs work harder at discouraging other students from endorsing such models, and gangs introduce more illegal activity to the school. The inability or unwillingness of adults in the school to do much about such behavior transforms the school. It makes the school less a haven, or place of safety, and more a sanctuary where law breakers enjoy immunity from arrest and prosecution for their crimes.

I do not know how many schools or school districts have deteriorated to this level, but I imagine that the situation I have described is common in many inner-city schools. The view of gangs and of schools in such places is far more consistent with popular and scientific folklore. Schools are seen as being largely irrelevant and not worthy of their students' respect or the community's support. Gangs members are seen as roving thugs. The best face to put on their behavior is to see them as primitive rebels acting out against bureaucratic carpetbaggers who represent an alien and hostile way of life.

This line of reasoning has real problems once one introduces the nasty reality of drug dealing and deadly violence into the equation. Nevertheless, the idea that gangs fill a social and moral hole in schools for a disfranchised urban peasantry has some utility. Gangs have been consistently portrayed as giving expression to the sour feelings held by neighborhood residents against outsiders such as unfriendly or unsympathetic school officials and social service workers.[24] Within the officially endorsed culture of the school, then, gangs might be seen as laying the groundwork for an alternative way of life that works for their neighbors and has, at least in the past, held open the possibility of defending some pretty conventional values.

Among the most prominent of these values would be loyalty to one's kin, whether real or fictive, an attachment to a neighborhood, and support for economic ventures that require the collaboration of friends and family members. Many people have observed that gangs often have a family-like quality. The idea that gangs serve as a substitute family for youngsters speaks to the continuing importance ascribed to the family as an institution by the gang members themselves. If we are to understand the significance of a substitute family for uprooted individuals, then it is crucial to appreciate that many immigrant peoples have used their rooming house, fraternal lodge, or church in much the same way as many youngsters use their gang.[25]

They helped newly arrived or unconnected persons to survive in an otherwise unfriendly urban world.

The sense of loyalty expressed by gang members for their neighborhood or "turf" is real, though not all gangs exhibit the same degree of attachment to their hometown. No matter how thin their attachment may be to a particular piece of land, such attachments are vital starting points in any campaign to build a more permanent community. The fact of being connected in an almost organic way to a piece of the urban landscape makes more credible any group's claim to being part of a real community with its own customs, beliefs, and folklore. Contemporary gangs could help make such claims, if their members treated local residents better. Here again we see an important way in which groups in the past have tried to build a place for themselves in a confusing and often hostile urban world and how groups in the present could make a similar contribution. Modern gangs find this difficult to accomplish, however, because of the drugs and violence they bring to their neighborhood.

Drugs and violence often are part of a neighborhood's economy when gangs are present, and this is another factor that limits the prospects for building healthy communities in these places. The ability of local residents to earn a living is important, but there are serious barriers to making successful neighborhood economies in many inner cities today. This has fed both the willingness of youths to engage in more criminal ventures for a longer period of time and the ferocity of their competition. Nevertheless, every gang member does not make money through illegal means in the same way or all the time. They may hold part-time jobs in the regular economy even though they depend on illegal enterprises for most of the money that they acquire.

The problem, as one young man described it, is that many of his peers had known little more than the streets and, as he put it, "workin' on the edges." If they were to make a lasting contribution to their town, they would have to move off the streets and find work that was less peripheral to the conventional economy. This would not be easy to do.

If the economies of neighborhoods in many cities and less well-to-do suburbs were better, there still would be room for a variety of part-time jobs in the non-conventional or illegal economy. We know from the history of entrepreneurial activities in many minority neighborhoods, and especially in black African and Caribbean communities, that illicit businesses held prominent spots in the local economy. The important point is that these illegal ventures would not occupy so important a spot in the thinking and early work experiences of young persons, if neighborhood economies were stronger. Moreover, the community would be able to withstand the incursion of individuals intent on behaving in ways that local residents could not accept.

In the meantime, it is interesting to note that contemporary youth gangs have reproduced collaborative ways to make money that other ethnic peoples have used in the past and still employ today. The most important of these techniques are rotating credit associations and mutual trade associations.[26] Gangs in the Fairview School District and elsewhere have adapted these techniques to fit their illegal drug trade.

People who form a rotating credit association, or RCA, usually do not have a great deal of money, and they try to multiply their buying power by cooperating with other individuals who are no better off than they are. Every member in the RCA places a modest sum of money into a common fund on a regular basis. Each member takes a turn drawing all or part of the money in the fund and spends it on an item or service that otherwise would be beyond his means to acquire. This arrangement continues until every member has had a chance to draw on the fund. Members can decide to disband the association, but not until everyone has benefited from it. Association members, who usually are friends or relatives, use the association to advance credit to each other. They assume that every person can be trusted to continue making their contributions, even after they have had their chance to draw on the fund.

Mutual trade associations, or MTAs, work differently. They consist of individual entrepreneurs who know each other and may even be members of the same extended family. These entrepreneurs compete vigorously within their trading territory or market area, but they will buy their products together in order to save money. They also will cooperate in defending their trading territory or market area when outsiders threaten to move into it. In this way, MTAs serve to limit the number of traders in an area and restrain the pricing and trading tactics that each member adopts.

Drug dealing that is undertaken by gangs combines features of rotating credit associations and mutual trade associations. Gang leaders will extend members credit so that they can buy their initial supply of drugs, and they will assign members specific trading areas and perhaps even train them. Gangs that are well organized sometimes create a "defense fund" to which everyone contributes. The money in this fund will be used to defray the legal costs of members who are arrested because of their drug dealing. Gangs will use the same wholesale distributor and will go to extreme lengths to protect their sales territory from other gangs. Gang members also act collaboratively when they extort money from businesses, burgle houses, steal cars, and fight. It is through such devices that the social and economic benefits of gang membership reinforce each other.

Parallels between the organized drug dealing done by gangs and more traditional ethnic enterprises are real, but gang members cannot realize all of the benefits offered by MTAs and RCAs. No matter how hard gang members try to act like older or experienced individuals, for instance, they are not adults. They cannot overcome the practical barriers to participating in the adult world more fully until they are older. They also pass in and out of the drug trade. They do not have a regular work and credit history that would take them into more conventional careers. Finally, their work puts them at the far edge of the economy. They cannot easily transfer their success into legitimate businesses.

It is for all these reasons that gangs are unlikely to provide their members with skills and experiences that enable them to move into the conventional economy. More gang members also will find it difficult to leave their marginal and criminal jobs because of economic conditions where they live. They will not be able to "mature out" of their gangbanging and assume more adult responsibilities as did gang members in earlier generations. It is not so easy for them to acquire a regular job, no matter how modest, and do those things that young men and women their age once did. They cannot easily establish work and credit histories, purchase and maintain their own home, marry and have children, or escape the tug of a reckless style of life. If they are lucky, they may be able to stand on the outskirts of what has come to be known as the "underclass." Unfortunately, they probably will not be able to escape its orbit.

The key to their success will not be to abandon gangs. Nor will it be to eradicate gangs, which is what most adults would like to do. The single most important thing that can be done is to make it easier for young men and women to "mature out" of gangs. This is the most effective way of reducing the amount of gang activity in a neighborhood, the degree of violence associated with it, and the dependence of gang members on jobs tied to criminal enterprises. It also happens to be a technique that has been used for many years by the gang members themselves.

Most experiments, counselling regimens, treatment innovations, internships, and training experiences for gang members that adults have parachuted into neighborhoods where gangs are found have worked poorly or not at all. The only gang intervention strategies to enjoy even marginal success have been those that made it possible for gang members to grow up and grow out of more active gang involvement. Many of the youngsters whom I interviewed had begun to figure this out for themselves, but they were not receiving much help from adults who were in their neighborhoods and schools. No one was making it easier for them to "mature out" of gangbanging. They had to do it all by themselves.

It was easier for the gang members of an earlier generation to move into conventional adult roles. There were more jobs available to them, more financially secure and stable families to anchor the community and to discipline young persons, and more groups and institutions in neighborhoods to help train young persons and integrate them into the adult world. Young men and women in many inner-city and suburban neighborhoods today are not similarly advantaged.

A successful gang intervention strategy will do nothing fancier than bring young persons back into conventional community groups, churches, schools, and family settings and then let those institutions do what they do best: build human beings. This is the most important lesson that students in the Fairview School District taught me.

This also will be the hardest thing for the rest of us to let happen, for it implies that we will not be in control of whatever is done in those communities. We may not trust the local adults enough to give them the assistance they need to pull it off. Or, we may doubt that there are enough of them to make their magic work. The result would be the same in either case.

We can find a way around this dilemma. In fact, we already have. Well-meaning people in the late nineteenth century invented something called a "settlement house." These houses were put in some of the most troubled neighborhoods that could be found in the cities of their day. Those who ran these places tried to serve as good role models for area residents and to provide services that local folks needed. These settlement houses did not work as well as their founders had hoped, and they certainly did not save all the local residents from their own bad habits or from the poverty that held them tightly. Yet the idea of seeding a troubled neighborhood with individuals and groups committed to staying there and making the place work better had much to recommend it. It still does.

I suggest that the United States already has the manpower and the means to make this work, and much of it is waiting in the several branches of our armed services. Men and women whose careers already have been marked by conspicuous public service await an early retirement as our military establishment is reduced in size. A proposal first made by retired Rear Admiral Norman Johnson of Boston University to put some of these persons to work in old military bases as teachers and mentors to inner-city youngsters has been picked up by other black leaders.[27] This is an excellent idea, but there is no reason why it could not be expanded to make retiring military personnel or police officers full-time residents in troubled neighborhoods and to offer them financial assistance to develop small businesses that will employ many of the youngsters they have helped to train.

What I propose is nothing less than the creation of thousands of settlement houses in the form of these small businesses.[28] The owners would put persons to work in their own neighborhoods and provide living examples of competent adults who will not leave the area or tolerate the poor behavior of the youngsters who live there. They also would constitute the first wave of a home-grown middle class for neighborhoods that other middle-class minorities have fled. It is unlikely that their presence would inspire persons who left such neighborhoods some time ago to return in large numbers. It is more likely that the availability of these new role models, middle-class mentors, or whatever they end up being called, would inspire other people to stay and make their community even more stable. The inclusion of such individuals in many inner-city neighborhoods would have a settling effect on everyone with whom they came into contact.

These new residents and businesses would not eradicate gangs or employ every young person who could use a job. They would not turn boys and girls doing bad things into angels. What they probably would do is curb some gang activities, employ more youngsters in local enterprises, and command the attention and respect of boys and girls of the area. Unlike the ambitious efforts of reformers during the 1960s to transform gangs into civil-rights organizations or legitimate businesses, this plan would give more responsibility and resources to the stable groups, institutions, and conventional adults who remain in the neighborhoods where gangs are found.

It was the youngsters in the Fairview School District who prompted me to think about their community and how they might be helped to fit into it better. They helped me to remember something else that is important as well. I was reminded that who I am and what I do are closely tied and make sense to me. These features merge in my mind and in the minds of others as a readily identifiable lump of a person who has been shaped by the rhythms and accumulated habits of four and a half decades of living. I am known by the ledger of my daily work.

These youngsters wish for nothing more than the chance to be known by the ledger of their daily work, and they search hard for opportunities to prove it. We would be well advised to heed their striving, and we would be well served if they could realize their wish in a more constructive fashion. Yet that probably will not happen. We are more likely to treat them as hopeless and undeserving of our attention, as not important enough to bring along. This may be comfortable for us and easy for them in the short term, but it does no one any good in the long run. All of us would be far better off, if we finally recognized these youngsters for what they really are: our children.

Notes

1 *Boston Globe*, November 6, 1993.
2 Ibid.
3 *St Louis Post-Dispatch*, April 30, 1993; May 1, 1993; May 2, 1993.
4 Joan Moore, "Gangs, Drugs, and Violence," in Scott Cummings and Daniel J. Monti (eds) *Gangs: the Origins and Impact of Contemporary Youth Gangs in the United States* (Albany, NY: State University of New York Press, 1993), p. 28.
5 Frederic M. Thrasher, *The Gang: a Study of 1,313 Gangs in Chicago* (Chicago: University of Chicago Press, 1927).
6 Gerald Suttles, *The Social Order of the Slum* (Chicago: University of Chicago Press, 1971); Diego Vigil, *Barrio Gangs: Street Life and Identity in Southern California* (Austin Tex.:

University of Texas Press, 1988); William Foote Whyte, *Street Corner Society: the Social Structure of an Italian Slum* (Chicago: University of Chicago Press, 1943).

7 L. Yablonsky. "The Delinquent Gang as a Near-Group," in M. Wolfgang (ed.) *The Sociology of Crime and Delinquency* (New York: John Wiley, 1962).

8 Martin Sanchez Jankowski, *Islands in the Street: Gangs and American Urban Society* (Berkeley, Calif.: University of California Press, 1991); James F. Short and Fred L. Strodtbeck *Group Process and Gang Delinquency* (Chicago: University of Chicago Press), pp. 106–9.

9 Daniel J. Monti "Origins and Problems of Gang Research in the United States," in Cummings and Monti, *Gangs*, p. 12.

10 Walter Miller, *Violence by youth Gangs and Youth Groups as a Crime Problem in Major American Cities*, National Institute for Juvenile Justice and Delinquency Prevention, Law Enforcement Assistance Administration, US Department Of Justice (Washington, DC: US Government Printing Office, 1975), p. 48; William Gale, *The Compound* (New York: Rawson Associates Publishers, 1977), p. 75.

11 Ray Hutchison and Charles Kyle, "Hispanic Street Gangs in Chicago's Public Schools," in Cummings and Monti, *Gangs*, pp. 113–36.

12 *New York Times*, July 24, 1993.

13 Arnold P. Goldstein and C. Ronald Huff (eds) *The Gang Intervention Handbook* (Champaign, Ill: Research Press, 1993).

14 Peter Berger and Richard John Neuhaus, *To Empower People: the Role of Mediating Structures in Public Policy* (Washington, DC: American Enterprise Institute for Public Policy Research, 1977); James F. Short, "Youth, Gangs and Society: Micro- and Macrosociological Processes," *The Sociological Quarterly* 15 (Winter 1974): pp. 3–19; James F. Short, "Politics and Youth Gangs: a Follow-up Study," *The Sociological Quarterly* 17 (Spring 1976): pp. 162–79.

15 Edwin Delattre, "Generous Understanding, Toleration, and the Liberal Arts," speech presented at Connecticut College, February 9, 1993.

16 Beryl Markham, *West With the Night* (San Francisco: North Point Press, 1983), p. 153.

17 J. Glenn Gray, *The Promise of Wisdom: a Philosophical Theory of Education* (New York: Harper Torchbooks, 1968), pp. 111, 112.

18 David Matza, *Delinquency and Drift* (New York: John Wiley, 1964).

19 Elijah Anderson, *Streetwise: Race, Class, and Change in an Urban Community* (Chicago: University of Chicago Press, 1990); John M. Hagedorn, *People and Folks: Gangs, Crime and the Underclass in a Rustbelt City* (Chicago: Lakeview Press, 1988); Joan Moore, *Going Down to the Barrio: Homeboys and Homegirls in Change* (Philadelphia, Pa.: Temple University Press, 1991); Mercer Sullivan, *"Getting Paid": Youth Crime and Work in the Inner City* (Ithaca, NY: Cornell University Press, 1989).

20 Ruth Horowitz, *Honor and the American Dream: Culture and Identity in a Chicano Community* (New Brunswick, NJ: Rutgers University Press, 1983); Jack Katz, *Seductions of Crime* (New York: Basic Books, 1988).

21 The term "culture" has been used in four ways, according to Raymond Williams. "First, 'culture' came to mean a 'a general state or habit of the mind,' with close relations to the idea of human perfection. Second, it came to mean 'a general state of intellectual and moral development in a society as a whole.' Third, it came to mean 'the general body of the arts and intellectual work.' Fourth, it came to mean 'the whole way of life, material, intellectual, and spiritual, of a given society' " (Raymond Williams, "Culture and Civilization," in Paul Edwards (ed.) *The Encyclopedia of Philosophy* (New York: Macmillan Publishing Co and The Free Press, 1967) vol. 1, p. 273.). It is in the last sense that social scientist typically think of the term "culture." My use of the term is different. I refer to culture as those organized ways of thinking and believing that persons use

to make sense of the world *and* those practices that enable persons to relate to the world as part of a collective enterprise. As such, I make room for the existence of multiple subcultures feeding into a larger, more diffuse culture. Other social scientists do the same. On the other hand, I also am offering up a view of culture that does not include a great deal of the clutter and noise that makes a brief or undistinguished appearance in our society. An idea or practice would have to make a substantial mark on society and contribute to the way large portions of the population made their way in the world before being considered a cultural good. Small things, such as a hula hoop or punk rock music, may be thought of as "fads" or they may last long enough to warrant our serious attention. Gangs are an important cultural phenomenon; they cannot be dismissed. However, not everything that gangs or gang members do and believe warrants serious attention or the mantle of legitimacy ascribed to it. Gangs do not offer a distinct way of life. They fit into the larger society, and they do so in ways that have been tried before and worked to varying degrees for the different peoples that have used them. Gangs cannot be accepted on their own terms, because many of the ideas and practices they follow are poor imitations of those found in the larger culture. Gangs also need not be studied or understood on their own terms for the same reason.

22 Jean Anyon, "Social Class and the Hidden Curriculum of Work," in Jeanne Ballantine (ed.) *Schools and Society* (Mountain View, Calif. Mayfield Publishing Company, 1989): pp. 257–79; Sally Lubeck, "Sandbox Society: Summary Analysis," in Ballantine, ibid., pp. 280–92.

23 J. Milton Yinger, "Contraculture and Subculture," *American Sociological Review*, October (1960): pp. 625–35; Ray Hutchison and Charles Kyle, "Gangs in School," in Cummings and Monti, *Gangs*, pp. 137–72.

24 Thrasher, *The Gang*.

25 Scott Cummings (ed.) *Self-Help in Urban America* (Port Washington, NY: Kennikat Press Corporation, 1986); Ivan Light, *Ethnic Enterprise in America* (Berkeley, Calif: University of California Press, 1972).

26 Carlos G. Velez-Ibanez, *Bonds of Mutual Trust* (New Brunswick, NJ: Rutgers University Press, 1983).

27 *Boston Globe*, January 8, 1994.

28 This approach to employing gang members would be different from that advocated by Arthur J. Ellis in his article "Urban Youth Economic Enterprise Zones: an Intervention Strategy for Reversing the Gang Crisis in American Cities" (*The Urban League Review* 15 (2), 1991–2, pp. 29–39). Ellis wants to train gang youths to become business owners and managers of a more conventional sort. He would have adult volunteers monitor their progress. I would make youths apprentices in businesses owned by full-time residents and entrepreneurs. Insofar as successful apprentices wanted to move on to become business owners in their own right, I certainly could support the kind of plan envisioned by Mr Ellis.

Index

killing, 47, 72–3, 122, 139
Kyle, Charles, 148

legitimate work, 11, 34, 56–9, 73,
 115, 119–21, 125, 127, 134,
 165, 167–9
Lord of the Flies, 27

Markham, Beryl, 158
Matza, David, 158
mediating structures, 154, 168
Milldale Boyz, 25, 35, 39, 42, 75–6
Milldale Girlz, 29–30, 75–6
military personnel, 168–9
Minister Don Muhammad, 132
Miller, Walter, 147
mutual trade associations, 114,
 166–7
Moore, Joan, 134–5, 137

National Association for the
 Advancement of Colored
 People, 134
National Urban Peace and Justice
 Summit, 134

Oakdales, 11–12, 25, 83, 86, 88,
 115–16, 126

Padilla, Felix, 155
pancaking, 10
parents, 7, 12–13, 15, 28, 31,
 34–6, 39, 41, 53, 62, 66, 70,
 79–82, 85, 118, 123–6, 128,
 140, 153, 156
peer culture, 162
perpetrator, 37, 67–8
Peter Pan, 27
Pine Ridge, 25, 41–2, 63–4, 83–4,
 86, 88

police, 12–14, 18, 31, 33, 72, 80,
 88, 105–6, 115–17, 153
punking, 32, 45, 90

Riveredge Posse, 25, 55, 73, 115–16
Rose Terrace, 11, 64, 87
Rose Terrace Boyz, 11
rotating credit association, 166–7

satanists, 97
scars, 67–8, 153
schools
 dropping out, 148
 as havens, 164
 hidden curriculum, 162
 staff, 5, 7, 18, 34, 41, 47–50, 57,
  63, 66, 87–8, 90, 92–4, 99,
  101, 105–6, 108–10, 123,
  125–6, 129, 143, 148, 164
 suspensions, 15, 63, 88, 91,
  93–4, 100, 105
settlement houses, 168–9
shoplifting, 30, 32, 111
space head, 13, 17

Thrasher, Frederic, 135–6, 138,
 140–1, 144, 146, 150, 154

underclass, 159, 167
Upchurch, Carl, 134
United States Commission on Civil
 Rights, 132

Vicelords, 12, 134, 152
Vista Village Boyz, 25, 39, 63–4,
 82, 87

wannabes, 10, 28, 31–2, 39, 45–6,
 65, 67, 73, 79, 127, 138
welfare checks, 116

NATIONAL UNIVERSITY LIBRARY LOS ANGELES

7740